First World War
and Army of Occupation
War Diary
France, Belgium and Germany

47 DIVISION
142 Infantry Brigade,
Brigade Trench Mortar Battery
20 March 1916 - 31 December 1918

WO95/2744/4

The Naval & Military Press Ltd
www.nmarchive.com
Published in association with The National Archives

Published by

The Naval & Military Press Ltd

Unit 10 Ridgewood Industrial Park,

Uckfield, East Sussex,

TN22 5QE England

Tel: +44 (0) 1825 749494

www.naval-military-press.com

www.nmarchive.com

This diary has been reprinted in facsimile from the original. Any imperfections are inevitably reproduced and the quality may fall short of modern type and cartographic standards.

© Crown Copyright
Images reproduced by permission of The National Archives, London, England, 2015.

Contents

Document type	Place/Title	Date From	Date To
Heading	WO95/2744 47 Div 142 Inf Bde Mar 16-Dec 18 Brigade Trench Mortar Battery		
Heading	47th Division 142nd Lt Trench Mortar Bty Mar 1916-Dec 1918		
Heading	142nd Brigade 47th Division 142nd Light Trench Mortar Battery 20th March To 31st July 1916		
Miscellaneous	D.A.G., 3rd Echelon, Base	01/09/1916	01/09/1916
War Diary	Fresnicourt	20/03/1916	21/03/1916
War Diary	Petit Servins	22/03/1916	26/03/1916
War Diary	Vimy Heights & Carency	27/03/1916	02/04/1916
War Diary	Petit Servins	03/04/1916	13/04/1916
War Diary	Carency & Vimy Heights	14/04/1916	20/04/1916
War Diary	Petit Servins	21/04/1916	30/04/1916
War Diary	Vimy Heights & Carency	02/05/1916	08/05/1916
War Diary	Petit Servins	09/05/1916	14/05/1916
War Diary	Vimy Heights & Carency	15/05/1916	20/05/1916
War Diary	Petit Servins	21/05/1916	21/05/1916
War Diary	Villers Au Bois	22/05/1916	22/05/1916
War Diary	Vimy Heights	23/05/1916	25/05/1916
War Diary	Petit Servins	26/05/1916	26/05/1916
War Diary	Divion	27/05/1916	12/06/1916
War Diary	Hersin	13/06/1916	16/06/1916
War Diary	Bully Grenay	17/06/1916	20/06/1916
War Diary	Hersin	21/06/1916	25/06/1916
War Diary	Aix Noulette	26/06/1916	30/07/1916
War Diary	Gavion	01/08/1916	03/08/1916
War Diary	Angres Sector & Bully Grenay	04/08/1916	14/08/1916
War Diary	Gavion	15/08/1916	16/08/1916
War Diary	Villers & Vimy	17/08/1916	27/08/1916
War Diary	Estree Cauchie	28/08/1916	28/08/1916
War Diary	Dieval	29/08/1916	30/08/1916
War Diary	Maizieres	31/08/1916	31/08/1916
War Diary	Lahoussoye	01/09/1916	09/09/1916
War Diary	Maxses Redoubt	10/09/1916	10/09/1916
War Diary	High Wood	11/09/1916	12/09/1916
War Diary	Fricourt Farm	20/09/1916	20/09/1916
War Diary	Blackwood	21/09/1916	21/09/1916
War Diary	Millencourt	22/09/1916	28/09/1916
War Diary	Mametz Wood	29/09/1916	30/09/1916
War Diary	High Wood & Bazentin Le Grand	13/09/1916	13/09/1916
War Diary	Fricourt Farm	14/09/1916	17/09/1916
War Diary	High Wood & Bazentin Le Grand	17/09/1916	19/09/1916
War Diary	Fricourt Farm	20/09/1916	20/09/1916
Operation(al) Order(s)	142 T.M.B Operation Order No. 1005	01/09/1916	01/09/1916
Miscellaneous	142 T.M.B Operation Orders	14/09/1916	14/09/1916
Miscellaneous	H X Operation Orders	17/09/1916	17/09/1916
Heading	142nd J.M.B		
Miscellaneous	War Diary 46 3rd Base Unit H.T. Depot A.S.C From 1.8.19 To 31.8.19		
War Diary	Mametz Wood	01/10/1916	01/10/1916

War Diary	(High Wood)	02/10/1916	09/10/1916
War Diary	Mametz Wood	10/10/1916	11/10/1916
War Diary	Lavieville	12/10/1916	15/10/1916
War Diary	Pont Remy	16/10/1916	16/10/1916
War Diary	Boeschepe	17/10/1916	19/10/1916
War Diary	Railway Dugouts Hill 60	20/10/1916	22/10/1916
War Diary	Hill 60 & Railway Dugouts	23/10/1916	31/10/1916
War Diary	Hill 60	01/11/1916	08/11/1916
War Diary	Devonshire Lines	09/11/1916	18/11/1916
War Diary	Canal Sub-Sector	19/11/1916	08/12/1916
War Diary	Devonshire Lines	09/12/1916	19/12/1916
War Diary	Hill 60 Sub Sector	20/12/1916	08/01/1917
War Diary	Devonshire Camp	09/01/1917	31/01/1917
War Diary	Canal Sub Sector	01/02/1917	03/02/1917
War Diary	Devonshire Lines	04/02/1917	11/02/1917
War Diary	Hill 60 Sub Sector	12/02/1917	28/02/1917
War Diary	Devonshire Camp	01/03/1917	07/03/1917
War Diary	Canal Sub Sector	08/03/1917	21/03/1917
War Diary	Devonshire Camp	22/03/1917	25/03/1917
War Diary	Ganspette	26/03/1917	09/04/1917
War Diary	Steenvoorde	10/04/1917	11/04/1917
War Diary	Devonshire Camp	12/04/1917	14/04/1917
War Diary	Canal Sub Sect	14/04/1917	27/04/1917
War Diary	Halifax Camp	28/04/1917	30/04/1917
War Diary	Halifax Camp (H.14)	01/05/1917	10/05/1917
War Diary	Canal Sub Sector	11/05/1917	24/05/1917
War Diary	Ottawa Camp	25/05/1917	01/06/1917
War Diary	Canal Sub Sector	02/06/1917	11/06/1917
War Diary	Westoutre	12/06/1917	15/06/1917
War Diary	Racquinghem	16/06/1917	26/06/1917
War Diary	(Sercus)	27/06/1917	30/06/1917
War Diary	Ridge Wood Wormezeele	01/07/1917	07/07/1917
War Diary	(Reninghelst)	08/07/1917	25/07/1917
War Diary	Westoutre	26/07/1917	01/08/1917
War Diary	(Aragon Camp)	02/08/1917	09/08/1917
War Diary	Moringhem	10/08/1917	17/08/1917
War Diary	Dominion Camp	18/08/1917	18/08/1917
War Diary	Pioneer Camp	19/08/1917	31/08/1917
War Diary	Ypres	01/09/1917	02/09/1917
War Diary	Scottish Lines	03/09/1917	05/09/1917
War Diary	Steenvoorde	06/09/1917	10/09/1917
War Diary	Dickebusch	11/09/1917	18/09/1917
War Diary	Sylvestre Cappel	19/09/1917	21/09/1917
War Diary	Maroeuil	22/09/1917	22/09/1917
War Diary	Anzin	23/09/1917	30/09/1917
War Diary	(Oppy Sector)	01/10/1917	10/10/1917
War Diary	St. Anzin	11/10/1917	18/10/1917
War Diary	(Gavrelle)	19/10/1917	05/11/1917
War Diary	Anzin	06/11/1917	13/11/1917
War Diary	Gavrelle	14/11/1917	18/11/1917
War Diary	Oppy	19/11/1917	19/11/1917
War Diary	St. Catherines	20/11/1917	20/11/1917
War Diary	Mt. St. Eloy	21/11/1917	21/11/1917
War Diary	Berneville	22/11/1917	27/11/1917
War Diary	Beaumetz Lez-Cambrai	28/11/1917	12/12/1917
War Diary	(Neuville)	13/12/1917	16/12/1917

War Diary	Henencourt	17/12/1917	04/01/1918
War Diary	Flesquieres Sector	05/01/1918	12/01/1918
War Diary	Bertincourt	13/01/1918	18/01/1918
War Diary	Humbercamps	18/01/1918	02/02/1918
War Diary	Bertincourt	03/02/1918	08/02/1918
War Diary	Flesquieres Right 5.5	09/02/1918	22/02/1918
War Diary	Bertincourt	23/02/1918	23/02/1918
War Diary	Rocquigny	24/02/1918	28/02/1918
Heading	142nd Inf. Bde. 47th Div. War Diary 142nd Trench Mortar Battery March 1918		
War Diary	Rocquigny	01/03/1918	20/03/1918
War Diary	Equancourt	21/03/1918	21/03/1918
War Diary	Neuville	22/03/1918	23/03/1918
War Diary	Lesboeufs	24/03/1918	24/03/1918
War Diary	Albert	25/03/1918	25/03/1918
War Diary	Millencourt	26/03/1918	26/03/1918
War Diary	Vauchelles	27/03/1918	27/03/1918
War Diary	Toutencourt	28/03/1918	29/03/1918
War Diary	Warloy	30/03/1918	31/03/1918
Heading	142nd Brigade 47th Division War Diary 142nd Trench Mortar Battery April 1918		
War Diary	Warloy	01/04/1918	01/04/1918
War Diary	Aveluy Wood	02/04/1918	06/04/1918
War Diary	Warloy	07/04/1918	08/04/1918
War Diary	Raincheval	09/04/1918	11/04/1918
War Diary	Montrelet	12/04/1918	12/04/1918
War Diary	Brailly	13/04/1918	28/04/1918
War Diary	Brucamp	29/04/1918	30/04/1918
War Diary	Warloy	01/05/1918	31/05/1918
War Diary	Baizieux	01/06/1918	21/06/1918
War Diary	Oissy	22/06/1918	18/07/1918
War Diary	Warloy	19/07/1918	30/07/1918
Heading	142nd Bde. 47th Div 142nd Trench Mortar Battery August 1918		
War Diary	Albert Sector	01/08/1918	05/08/1918
War Diary	Warloy	06/08/1918	20/08/1918
War Diary	Heilly	21/08/1918	28/08/1918
War Diary	Hardicourt	30/08/1918	31/08/1918
Miscellaneous	Appendix No.1 To War Diary		
War Diary		01/09/1918	08/09/1918
War Diary	Mericourt	09/09/1918	10/09/1918
War Diary	Ecquedecques	11/09/1918	12/09/1918
War Diary	Allouagne	13/09/1918	19/09/1918
War Diary	Antin	20/09/1918	27/09/1918
War Diary	Pronay	28/09/1918	30/09/1918
Miscellaneous	142 T.M.B Summary Of Operations From 5.30 am to 4.0 pm Sept 1st 1918	01/09/1918	01/09/1918
War Diary	Pronay	01/10/1918	04/10/1918
War Diary	Fromelles	05/10/1918	14/10/1918
War Diary	Radingham	15/10/1918	18/10/1918
War Diary	Bourecq	19/10/1918	26/10/1918
War Diary	Loos	27/10/1918	31/10/1918
War Diary	Willems	01/11/1918	06/11/1918
War Diary	Templeuve	07/11/1918	08/11/1918
War Diary	Kain	09/11/1918	09/11/1918
War Diary	Frasnes	10/11/1918	10/11/1918

War Diary	Kain	11/11/1918	13/11/1918
War Diary	Tournai	14/11/1918	22/11/1918
War Diary	Cysoing	23/11/1918	24/11/1918
War Diary	Haubourdin	25/11/1918	25/11/1918
War Diary	Bethune	26/11/1918	26/11/1918
War Diary	Allouagne	27/11/1918	31/12/1918

WO 95/2744 (4)

47 Div   142 Inf Bde

Mar '16 — Dec '18

   Brigade Trench Mortar Battery

47TH DIVISION

142ND LT TRENCH MORTAR BTY

MAR 1916-DEC 1918

142nd Brigade.
47th Division.

142nd LIGHT TRENCH MORTAR BATTERY

20th MARCH to 31st JULY 1916.

Dec '18

D. A. G.,

    3rd. Echelon,

        Base.

    Herewith War Diary please for the 142nd. Trench Mortar Battery for the period March/July 1916.

                                    Captain,
                                  a/Staff Captain,
                                  142nd. Inf. Bde.

HEADQUARTERS 142nd INFANTRY BRIGADE — No. C.581/3 — Date 1/9/16.

Army Form C. 2118.

WAR DIARY
or
INTELLIGENCE SUMMARY.
(Erase heading not required.)

Instructions regarding War Diaries and Intelligence Summaries are contained in F. S. Regs., Part II and the Staff Manual respectively. Title pages will be prepared in manuscript.

Place	Date	Hour	Summary of Events and Information	Remarks and references to Appendices
	1916			
Etroncourt	20.3		Battery reorganised. Two batteries formed. No. 2 was 143 & 144 Light Mortar Battery. Total strength each 4 officers 50	*See 6 S.I.S culls date being tried has been issued as attack was not made
"	21.3	9 a.m	Moved to Petit Servins	
Petit Servins	22.3		Cleaning up. Oaks & trucks	
"	23.3		" "	
"	24.3		Very snowy. Lectures	
"	25.3		Practice firing with 3.7" mortars	
"	26.3		Church parade	
Vimy Heights & Carency	27.3		Moved 1 section into the line on Vimy heights, 1 section in reserve billets at Carency	
"	28.3		Fairly fine - strong wind. Usual routine of the line	
"	29.3		Registration carried out & emplacements dug	
"	30.3		Very fine. G. aircraft active	
"	31.3		Hostile aircraft very active. weather beautiful	
"	1.4		Situation normal	
"	2.4		Relieved from the line by 141 Bde & moved back to Petit Servins	
Petit Servins	3.4		Rested. Working party from 7 p.m. to 3 a.m. work on Maistre Line	

WAR DIARY or INTELLIGENCE SUMMARY.

Army Form C. 2118.

(Erase heading not required.)

Instructions regarding War Diaries and Intelligence Summaries are contained in F.S. Regns., Part II. and the Staff Manual respectively. Title pages will be prepared in manuscript.

Hour, Date, Place	Summary of Events and Information	Remarks and references to Appendices
Petit Servins 4.4.916.	Wall cold.	
5	"	
6	Working party from 7 p.m. to 2 a.m. took on marker line at Lavency	
7		
8		
9		
10		
11		
12		
13	Lotting training.	
14		
Carency Knight 15		
16	Moves to line, one section to Carency.	
17		
18	Usual routine.	
19		
Petit Servins 20	Heavy fire a reply to our reprisals. 11 p.m. Enemy heavy bombard on SP 20	
21		
22	Relieved from line. Relieved by 1/4 Batt.	
23	Road cleaning &c.	
24	No 4 windy. Drill &c.	
25	Fire. Gun drill. Church parade	
26	Bath at Bouvicourt no clean clothes. Gun drill 2-4. p.m.	
27	Usual training firing 2-7.15 p.m.	
28	Usual training	
29	4 Stokes fifthy Demonstration at back of shrol &c. Stokes 3" Mortar.	

(73989) W4141–463. 400,000. 9/14. H.&J.Ltd. Forms/C. 2118/10.

Army Form C. 2118.

WAR DIARY
or
INTELLIGENCE SUMMARY.
(Erase heading not required.)

Instructions regarding War Diaries and Intelligence Summaries are contained in F.S. Regs., Part II. and the Staff Manual respectively. Title pages will be prepared in manuscript.

Hour, Date, Place	Summary of Events and Information	Remarks and references to Appendices
Petit Servins 30.4.16.	Brig General Inspection Chief found Satisfied a number of faults from in.	
Vimy Heights 1.5.	Returned to the line.	
Carency 2.		
3.	Covering fire when 3 craters met up. Good results	
4.5.6.	Usual numbers	
5.7	Relieved to Bonet Minenwerfer	
8	Relieved by 141 Bde an Petit Servins 5 pm	
Petit Servins 9.5.16	Clean up, Rifle inspection etc	
10.5.16	Batt'n fog parades	
11	Usual thing	
12	— N —	
13		
14	Lecture	
Vimy Heights 15	Moved into line, relieved 140 Bde. (Our Section in line at Carency)	
Pt Carency 16		
17	Sine.	
18	Schians escaped over	
19	Hy Hostile arty active, had all night work on new positions	
20	Minenwerfer very active	
	Hy shelling heavily. Relieved by 141. Bde. Returned to Petit Servins	
Petit Servins 21.	Training.	
Villers au Bois ≡	Batt'n turned to Villers au Bois.	
22	Stood to Avoiding order.	
Vimy Heights 23	Drew 1 days rations. To find line. Took over from 140 Bde with 2 Stokes 3" Built one position and another gun	

C. J. Clemow
C/o 14[?]th M.B.
O.C. 142[?] M.B.

Army Form C. 2118.

WAR DIARY
or
INTELLIGENCE SUMMARY.
(Erase heading not required.)

Instructions regarding War Diaries and Intelligence Summaries are contained in F.S. Regs., Part II and the Staff Manual respectively. Title pages will be prepared in manuscript.

Hour, Date, Place	Summary of Events and Information	Remarks and references to Appendices
Vimy Heights. 22.5.916	(cont) Attack by 21st Lond Regt & 24th Lond Regt assisted by our rapid fire. Sap head established by us. Hostile bomb store blown up.	
24	Vengeful Surprises for Fritz.	
25	Relieved at 10 pm by Gro Div. Three casualties in course of to billets at Petit Servins. Returned	
Petit Servins 26	Marched to Sains.	
Sains 27	Cleaned up etc.	
28	Inspection by Gen Monro.	
29 – to 7 July 12	Manual & Battery training. On June 7 Lt Mowbray took charge of the 141 Battery. The two batteries were combined into one battery with two sections.	
	Moved to Hersin.	
Hersin 13 to 16	Manual training.	
Bully Grenay 17	Moved to Bully Grenay. One section relieved 141 TMB in Angres sector	
	Usual line routine	
18 – 20	Relieved by 141 TMB & moved to Gavron.	
21.	Manual training.	
Hersin 22 – 24	Moved to Aix Noulette. One section to the line.	
25	Making up ammunition (large quantities)	
Aix Noulette 26	Terrific bombardment to our [?] to 141 Td Angres sector who were making a raid.	
27	Usual routine	
28.29		

Army Form C. 2118.

WAR DIARY
or
INTELLIGENCE SUMMARY.
(Erase heading not required.)

Instructions regarding War Diaries and Intelligence Summaries are contained in F.S. Regs., Part II and the Staff Manual respectively. Title pages will be prepared in manuscript.

Hour, Date, Place		Summary of Events and Information	Remarks and references to Appendices
Our Nouvelle	30.7.16	Relieved by 140 T.M.B. Returned to Gavion.	
Gavion	1 – 2.8.16	Usual routine	
	3	Returned to Angres Sector	
Angres sector of Bully Grenay	4	Usual routine	
	5	Covering fire to 140 Bde in Souchez sector for their raid.	
	6, 7	Quiet.	
	8	1000 rounds ammn expended during enemy's raid by 22nd London Regt. One gun with op. site 300 rounds.	
		One casualty.	
	9–13	Usual line routine.	
	14	Relieved by R.N.D. – to Gavion	
Gavion	15	Usual routine	
	16	Moved to Villers au Bois. 1 section in line on Vimy heights	
Villers 4 Vimy	17–26	Usual line routine. On 21st Kemps T.M. strafe again.	
		hostile minenwerfer.	
	27	Relieved by 37th Div. 1 proceeded to Estrée-Cauchie	
Estrée-Cauchie	28	Moved to Dieval. Bus out of Bde column owing to having no available transport. Arrived 11. P.M	
Dieval	29	Rested etc.	
	30	Proceeded to Mazières at 3.0 a.m and 9.30 a.m. 22nd London Regt provided 33 men to help pull transport.	
Mazières	31	Rested.	

C. E. Cooper
Major
O.C. 142nd T.M.B.

(73989) W4141–463. 400,000. 9/14. H.&J.Ltd. Forms/C. 2118/10.

Army Form C. 2118.

142 T.M. Bty
Vol 7

WAR DIARY
or
INTELLIGENCE SUMMARY
(Erase heading not required.)

Instructions regarding War Diaries and Intelligence Summaries are contained in F. S. Regs., Part II. and the Staff Manual respectively. Title pages will be prepared in manuscript.

Place	Date	Hour	Summary of Events and Information	Remarks and references to Appendices
LAHOUSSOYE	Sept. 1		Coys. Physical drill. Battery gun drill. Emplacement building. Preparations for Operations. Field operations. (00.1005). Cleaning gear, harness. Repairs to harness.	Appendix I. of Approach
	2		Bull. Church parade.	
	3		Physical drill. Heavy rain caused parade to be postponed. Rifle practice trenches reoccupd. after.	
	4		Sims. Worked in battery ads. One gun firing demonstration. 122 rounds fired.	
	5		Gas helmet test at Div. Gas School. (30.0.5.) Interior economy + Lecture on Stokes 3" mortar.	
	6		Sims. Physical training. Route march. (F.M.O.) Mutual instruction + lecture.	
	7		"	
	8		Close order drill + battery drill.	
	9		Phys. drill. Squad + gun drill. Lecture + gas helmet practice.	
MAXSES REDOUBT	10	9.15.a.m	Moved to MAXSES REDOUBT (ALBERT-BÉCOURT road) arr. 2.15. 8 mortars + officers' kits taken by motor lorry. Two off tents take over. O.R. bivouaced.	
HIGH WOOD.	11	5.15.a.m	Drive. Moved with 8 mortars to relieve 2 T.M.B. at HIGH WOOD. Stopped oker gear at LANCART, at horse lines. HQs at BAZENTIN LE GRAND (Map Ref. ALBERT, (ab000 S.15.b.3.6). Relief 9.a.m. Fired 100 rounds wounded O.R.3.	
	12		Sims. One section withdrawn to reserve line until emplacements could be built. Collecting T.M. ammo. which was found to have been stored by shell fire. Consolidated emplacement, hindered by heavy shell fire. Auxiliary positions built. Lieut. G.F. Camm. to F.Amb. suffering from shell shock. Wounded O.R. 1.	

Army Form C. 2118.

WAR DIARY
or
INTELLIGENCE SUMMARY.
(Erase heading not required.)

Place	Date	Hour	Summary of Events and Information	Remarks and references to Appendices
FRICOURT FARM	Sept 20		(Continued) Bivouacked. Left area at 5.30 p.m. to BLACKWOOD. 8.15 p.m. Three b.ts. O.R. bivouaced.	
BLACKWOOD	21		Left BLACKWOOD at 10.45 a.m. am MILLENCOURT 1.0 p.m. Heavy going with few laden horses. Billeted.	
MILLENCOURT	22		Fine. Refitting, cleaning up kit, few notices. Land carts in tow ecorary.	
	23		" Ball.	
	24, 5		" Church parade. Squad + battery drill. Lecture	
	26		" Gyro drill. Instruction to new men. Gun + squad drill. Route march	
	(27)			
	28		Wet. Enl. Inspection. Moved at 2.30 p.m. to MAMETZ WOOD (X.24.a.74 ALBERT SHEET 1/40.000)	
			Arrived 7.45 p.m. Took over dugouts + shelters from 141 T.M.B. at 5 a.m. 29th Sept. Most difficult	
			moving with T.M. trucks through wood.	
MAMETZ WOOD	29		Wet. Roads + tracks very bad. Fatigues etc.	
	30		Fine + drying. Roads etc. much improved. Improved shelters.	

E. Potts
Lieut

[stamp: 142 TRENCH MORTAR BATTERY. No. ... Date 30.9.16]

Army Form C. 2118.

WAR DIARY
or
INTELLIGENCE SUMMARY.
(Erase heading not required.)

Instructions regarding War Diaries and Intelligence
Summaries are contained in F. S. Regs., Part II.
and the Staff Manual respectively. Title pages
will be prepared in manuscript.

Place	Date	Hour	Summary of Events and Information	Remarks and references to Appendices
	Sept.			
HIGH WOOD & BAZENTIN le GRAND	13.		Shoring work on positions, consolidating, sandbags etc. Hindered by heavy shell fire. 1 mortar out of action. Section charges over. Relieved mortar destroyed. 6 rounds fired. Wounded O.R. 1	
	14.		Kept fire relieved by 140, 141 T.M.B.S. 7.30 complete. Moved to 57.D.S.E.-X.28.c.6.7. Bivouaced in FRICOURT FARM. (Officers included) 1 Officer (24th LOND RGT) attached to battery. One load out of 4. Others in moving wounded O.R. 2	
	15.		B.E.D. Deville Wood to our day. Moved at 11. P.M. to BAZENTIN le GRAND arrived 2 a.m. (L.Q.U.) Heavy firing. One officer (21st LOND. REGT) to hospital. Extra ammunition issued	Appendix II
			with 6 carts. Erected ground sheet shelters to break. do. for H.S. & officers. One action relieved	
	17		144 T.M.G. as One action worked partly. Reserve lines fiercely shelled Sunk Lewis gun sheets.	
HIGH WOOD & BAZENTIN le GRAND			Relief complete 1.15. A.M. Re-organised positions and consolidated. Team shells in reserve lines. No. 1 section took our positions. No. 2 formed a working party. No. 2 returned to reserves in evening.	Appendix III
	18		At dawn No. 1 moved forward in front of HIGH WOOD. Withdrew to BEDFORD TRENCH in evening. Very heavily bombarded by enemy. No. 2 section moved up to C.O. line. Relief carried partly & over forward. was over O.P.2.	
	19.		Two teams with mortars advanced to STARFISH REDOUBT (under C.O. 22nd LOND. REGT) at 11.30 a.m. Remaining teams stayed at BEDFORD TRENCH Post. w. 40 boxes S.A.A. moved forward with two teams. Relieved by 1st Div. at 2.0 a.m. Detached action from forward positions relieved at 5 a.m. Wounded 3.	
FRICOURT FARM	20		Arrived at FRICOURT FARM at 8 a.m. "absolutely exhausted". Guns taken from BAZENTIN LE GRAND through aboriginal roads, caused by wet weather. Detached teams carried all guns & ammunition from positions to FRICOURT FARM. (continued)	

2333 Wt. W 2341/1454 700,000 5/15 D. D. & L. A.D.S.S./Forms/C.2118.

APPENDIX I

SECRET.   COPY No 2

142 T.M.B.

OPERATION ORDER No 1005

REF. SPECIAL MAP.   SEPT. 1. 1916

1. 142nd Inf Bde — in conjunction with
140th & 141st Inf Bde — has been ordered
to take enemy's front line & immediate
support trenches between A & B on a
date to be notified later.
141st Bde on the left. 140th in support.
142nd on right.
50th Division on right of 142. Inf Bde.

2. Objective for Brigade.
To take & consolidate enemy front line &
support trenches between points —
I.1.d.4.6, & I.1.c.4.3

3. Dispositions:
(a) O/c No 1 section. 142 T.M.B. will
co-operate with 23rd Lond
(Right attack) — {H.Q. I.1.c.4.3}
(b) O/c No 2 section. 142 T.M.B. will
co operate with 22nd Lond — (Left attack)
— {H.Q. H.6.D.8.a.}

4. Assault will be delivered at Zero

5. The O.i/c. sections 1&2 T.M.B. will report to O.C. concerned at ZERO minus 60.

6. All guns will fire bursts of rapid fire — from time to time — & keep up a slow bombardment of the enemy front line — for 24 hours before ZERO.

7. At Zero minus 3 — all guns will fire rapid on enemy front line, ~~Continue~~ until ZERO minus 1 — when —

(a) 2 guns per section will increase their range & fire on support line — until the attacking troops to advance from the captured enemy front line & enemy support line.

(b) The remaining two guns per section will cease firing at ZERO minus 1 — & prepare to advance with their respective attacks.
(Arrangements as to when guns advance to be made with Bn. commanders)

8. When enemy front line has been taken & consolidated & the attack is being pushed on — the two guns per section (Para. 7(a)) — will advance to give

covering fire to the advance — take up
positions in readiness for any counter attack.

9. Ammunition Supply:

There will be four dumps in
'RED FLAG TR~~ench~~' — at
(a) E in R<u>E</u>D
(b) A in FL<u>A</u>G
(c) R in T<u>R</u>
(d) P in CRO<u>P</u>

Each dump will consist of 300 rounds.

O/c sections must arrange for the
carrying of ammunition from these
dumps to advanced positions of guns.

Each dump will be supplied from
Adv. Report Centre dump — & the O.C.
142 T.M.B. will hold himself
responsible for this.

10. MEDICAL. Advanced Dressing Station
— H.12.a.7.5.
Walking Cases will go to Pont. Noyelles.

11. Advanced Report Centre. H.12.a.5.21.

12. In case of casualties occurring — reinforcements will be at Advanced Report Centre.

            Geo L Camm
                Lieut
            OC. 142. T.M.B.

Issued at 11.0 am. to O/c. sections T.M.B.

COPY No. 1.   File
          2.   WAR DIARY
          3.   142. Inf Bde.
          4.   O/c. No 1 sec. T.M.B.
          5.   "   " 2   "

NOTES.

ZERO.   9.0 am   Sept. 2. 1916

The 142. T.M.B. will not fire live ammo. The enemy will be represented by a skeleton coy. without steel helmets. Barrage by Red Flags.

SECRET.   APPENDIX II   COPY Nº 1.

142 T M B
OPERATION ORDERS

Ref: Special Map & Sheets
57c S.W & 57d S.E.   14 Sept 1916

1. The Fourth Army will attack tomorrow at 6.20 am between COMBLES and MARTINPUICH. The New Zealand Div. on right, 50th Div. on left.

2. The 140 Inf. Bde on right, 141st Inf. Bde on left; & 142 Inf. Bde in reserve.

3. The Div¹. attacking area is between True Bearings 31½° and 46°.
   First Objective: S 3 b 9.8 — S 5 a 7.3
   Second do.   : M 34 b 3.2 — M 35 d 5.6
   Third do   : M 34 b 8.8 — M 36 a 4.0

4. Each objective will be consolidated as soon as captured. Strong points will be constructed as under:—
   (1) S 5 c 2.7
   (2) S 4 b 5 4
   (3) STARFISH (2nd objective)
   (4) M 34 d. 1.1
   (5) S 3 b 9½.7
   (6) M 34 d. 8. 9

5. Detail of Maps to be carried. All officers to be in possession of the following maps:—

FRANCE - Sheet 57c N.W
" 57c S.W.
" 57d S.E.
LENS II. scale 1/100,000.

6. Fighting Order will be worn. No letters, documents or papers which might convey information of military value will be carried. Officers will carry no public money.

7. Bde Headquarters will be at X 30 a 5.7

8. <u>Dumps</u>
   S. 3 d. 6. 9
   S. 9 b. 8. 9
   S. 4 c. 2 4

9. <u>Medical</u>
   Aid Posts will be established at
   ELGIN AVE - S 9 d. 4. 2
   HIGH ALLEY - S 9 c 9. 2

   [signature]
   Lieut
   for OC 142 T.M.B.

Copy No 1 - File
     2 - War Diary
     3 - Bde
     4 - OC No 1 Section
     5 - OC No 2 Section

SECRET APPENDIX III COPY Nº
        H X
        OPERATION ORDERS

Ref. Special Map   17 Sept 1916

1. Bde will capture & consolidate line G to E, and also consolidate R to O joining up gap near F.

2. TMB will be prepared to carry up two mortars in STAR FISH LINE and will get into communication with O's C concerned – Two teams from Nº 2 Section to go forward.

3. 22 LON. will seize & consolidate P to R and from F to G.
   24 LON. will seize & consolidate O to P and E to F.

4. Carrying parties will report to OC Nº 2 Section & be prepared to take up ammunition when mortars advance to STAR FISH LINE.

5. Nº 1 Section will advance & take over Nº 2 Section's mortars.

6. There will be no artillery bombardment & infantry & TMB will advance as quickly as possible – STAR FISH LINE reported to be held very weakly if at all.

7. Advance to be timed so that leading troops enter E to G at 3 am.

8. Strong Points to be made at M 34 d. 9. 7 and near O.

                                    E S Piters
                                      Lieut
11 pm

142 — J.M.B.

Volume No.

BRITISH SALONIKA FORCE

WAR DIARY.

		PERIOD	
Vol. No.	Unit	From	To
46.	3rd Base H.T. Depot. A.S.C.	1.8.19	31.8.19
35.	29th Reserve Park. R.A.S.C.	1.8.19	31.8.19
29.	800 H.T. Coy. R.A.S.C.		

Army Form C. 2118.

142nd T.M. Battery Vol 1

WAR DIARY
or
INTELLIGENCE SUMMARY.
(Erase heading not required.)

Instructions regarding War Diaries and Intelligence Summaries are contained in F. S. Regs., Part II. and the Staff Manual respectively. Title pages will be prepared in manuscript.

Place	Date	Hour	Summary of Events and Information	Remarks and references to Appendices
MAMETZ WOOD	Oct. 1		Fine. Moved about 9.30 a.m. to HIGHWOOD Sector (C.O.14.) HQ at BAZENTIN LE GRAND cross-roads.	
(HIGH WOOD)	2		Wet. Usual line routine. Reserve section in line. Four in reserve at CRUCIFIX CORNER.	
	3		Wet. Reserve section moved to HIGH WOOD with 3 mortars.	
	4		Nil. Situation of ammunition to half-way dump, stores etc. Motors mounted on defensive scheme.	
	5		Fine. Draying. Line routine. Strengthened and built stores, sides of position etc.	
	6		Fine	
	7		Fine. Supported attack by MO.K.T.B. (on offensive lines) (Operation Order N° 118.)	
	8		Line routine. Prepared ammunition; salvage work.	
	9		Fine. Relieved by South African Troop. (C.O.O. N° 120) moved to MAMETZ WOOD. Extreme difficulty of moving hand-tramways at recoiled gear etc. owing to [?] on road-side mud frequent. Roads almost impossible for hand-drawn transport.	
MAMETZ WOOD.	10		Fine. Gen. picked up by motor lorry. Rotting with hand-carts moved to LAVIEVILLE. (Am: 6.30 p.m.) Took over five tents as accommodation. (OD 12.)	
	11		Fine. Cleaned up gear, equipment etc. Inspection by O.C.	

Army Form C. 2118.

WAR DIARY
or
INTELLIGENCE SUMMARY.
(Erase heading not required.)

Instructions regarding War Diaries and Intelligence Summaries are contained in F. S. Regs. Part II. and the Staff Manual respectively. Title pages will be prepared in manuscript.

Place	Date	Hour	Summary of Events and Information	Remarks and references to Appendices
LAVIEVILLE	12 (Oct)		Pre Emp General Inspection, Parade stand by force	
	13		General inspection OC Bakery force (Col BAZIN)	
	14		Bn moved with all force to ALBERT Entrained and loaded traffic	
		1.0 p.m.	(C.O.O. No 23.)	
	15		Detrained at GODEWAERSVELDE — moved by road with transports to await	
			arrival Pont Remy 2.0 p.m. Billeted in loft near station	
PONT REMY	16		30 road (all ready) 3.45 a.m. Entrained — arrived LONGPRÉ c. 5.50 p.m. dry road	
			to BOESCHÈPE (arr. c. 6 p.m.) Billett — loft.	
BOESCHÈPE	17		Divie. Clean up, gear etc.	
	18		Wet. Inspection etc.	
	19		Wet. Gear and personal escort by Bae lorries to HUEGATE TIMES. Remainder for	
			to RAILWAY DUGOUTS (Cav. E. Fins) One section relieves 6th Aust T.M.B. in line (O.O. 015)	
RAILWAY DUGOUTS — HILL 60	20		Broad. Divie. Handcarts parked in TRANSPORT FARM. Relation to hostile gun	
			T.M. activity. Work of strengthening oc command on Afognana.	
	21		Divie. cold. Two further gun positions Lem full. School of ammn. at	
	22		Divie. work on gun positions continued. No range fired on hostile work.	

Army Form C. 2118.

WAR DIARY
or
INTELLIGENCE SUMMARY.
(Erase heading not required.)

Instructions regarding War Diaries and Intelligence Summaries are contained in F. S. Regs., Part II. and the Staff Manual respectively. Title pages will be prepared in manuscript.

Place	Date	Hour	Summary of Events and Information	Remarks and references to Appendices
HILL 60 & RAILWAY DUGOUTS	Oct. 23.		Dull, mild. 30 rounds fired in retaliation to enemy T.M. activity. Defences approaches to gun positions etc.	
			Recom. section formed working party.	
	24		Wet. Retaine section stood down. 170 rounds fired.	
	25		Wet. Hostile T.M.s very active. Since 2.05 rounds in retaliation. Reconst. working party.	
	26		" Sixty pumps are aunts put to drainage of gun positions.	
	27		Situation normal. Draining and other work continued.	
	28		No 2 gun team out of action owing to premature shell burst through jam of fly off lever. No casualties.	
	29		No 1 section relieved in line by No 2 section. 210 rounds fired.	
	30		Unit this took downer on T.M. 110 rounds fired to noon (30.10.16)	
	31		In conjunction with artillery, Battery carried out a searching bombardment of the enemys front line system throughout the night. 393 r.d.(C.D. RS.2) 218 rounds fired on targets and traversing trenches.	

[signature]
O.C. 142 T.M.B.

142nd T.M. Bty

2nd TRENCH MORTAR BATTERY
30.11.16

WAR DIARY
or
INTELLIGENCE SUMMARY
(Erase heading not required.)

Army Form C. 2118

Instructions regarding War Diaries and Intelligence Summaries are contained in F. S. Regs., Part II. and the Staff Manual respectively. Title pages will be prepared in manuscript.

Place	Date	Hour	Summary of Events and Information	Remarks and references to Appendices
"Hill 60"	Nov. 1		Fired 87 rounds against hostile works & wire damaged.	
	2		ditto 300 " " " and Min=enwerfer. Huns damage reported.	
	3		No 1 section relieved No 2 do. Situation normal. Work on gun positions	
	4		O.O. 129 carried out. 106 mm fired in retaliation to T.M. activity. No 6 gun position damaged slightly by blowing of our camouflet. Repairs to positions executed.	
	5		Fine. Hostile mortar emplacement fired upon w. good results. New reserve position finished. Detonating the shells in reserve area.	
	6		Fine. Work on reserve dug outs. Detonator 39 cas fired against hostile T.M. empl.	
	7		Situation quiet. Usual line routine and work in reserve area.	
	8		Relieved by 140 T.M.B. 5.30 p.m. (O.O.131) Moved with 7 handcarts to DEVONSHIRE LINES arr. c. 10.0. p.m. Took over 5 huts. Condition of camp - bad. Wet.	
DEVONSHIRE LINES	9		Fine. Cleaning equipment, gear &c.	
	10		Clean inspection - equipment do. Small kit inspection.	
	11		" " " Narrows. Gunn. Interior economy.	
	12		Party to presentation of honour ribbons. Respirator drill and practice.	
	13		Physical, close order, gun, respirator drills. Route march.	

Army Form C. 2118.

WAR DIARY
or
INTELLIGENCE SUMMARY
(Erase heading not required.)

[Stamp: 142nd TRENCH MORTAR BATTERY. 30.11.16.]

Place	Date	Hour	Summary of Events and Information	Remarks and references to Appendices
DEVONSHIRE LINES.	Nov. 14		Dull. Physical instruction by B.S.F.O. to battery. Gun drill. Cleaning billets.	
	15		Recruits class. Gun drill. Lecture. General work of importance to camp.	
	16		Instruction in stores. Gun drill, close order drill in. Recreation - football.	
	17		TO HOPOUTRE for bath. Clean changes of underlinen.	
	18		Relieved 141 T.M.B. in CANAL SUB-SECTOR. (A.O. 132.) Reserve section in HODGE WALK. BEDFORD HOUSE.	
CANAL SUB-SECTOR.	19		Dull. Situation quiet. Work on positions etc.	
	20		30 rds fired in 'retaliation'.	
	21		Dull. Ranging of positions attended to. Registration.	
	22		(One) thirty Detonating and usual line routine.	
	23		Registered on hostile wire for wire-cutting experiment. Dr NATUN. S.W. wounded (bullet).	
	24		Considerable T.M. (hostile) activity during afternoon. 106 rds fired in retaliation. Work on bomb stores.	
	25		Working party of reserve section to line. Strengthening positions and distribution of ammo.	
	26		Situation normal. Firing to schedule. Carried out blanking night.	
	27		Usual line routine. Work on reserve area dug-outs etc.	
	28		Dull misty. Situation quiet. N°2 Sub. relieved N°1 do. in line.	
	29, 30		Usual line routine. Work in reserve dug-outs.	

Army Form C. 2118.

WAR DIARY
or
INTELLIGENCE SUMMARY
(Erase heading not required.)

142nd T.M. Battery
Vol 10

Place	Date	Hour	Summary of Events and Information	Remarks and references to Appendices
CANAL SUB-SECTOR	Dec. 1		Fine. Work on reserve dug-outs. Salvage work. Usual line routine. Ammo. to new positions.	
	2		Dull. " " " " "	
	3		" " , drawing etc.	
	4		Two positions damaged by hostile T.M. fire.	
	5		Fine. 100 rds fired in retaliation. Hostile registering on reserve area. 1 Mk II mounting in BEDFORD HO. out of actn.	
	6		(Fair) 102 " " " " "	
	7		" " " " Shelling	
	8		Detonating of ammo and usual work on emplacements etc.	
	9		Misty early. Fine. Situation quiet. Work	
	10		Battery relieved by 140 T.M.B. Moved to DEVONSHIRE LINES (BUSSEBOOM) arr. 8.0.p.m. — took over 6 huts.	
DEVONSHIRE LINES	9		Gear, kit and equipment cleaned up.	
	10		Attendance at Div. Commander's presentation of Ribbons at 'VAUXHALL'. Remainder of Battery to Church parade. One hut handed over to 24th LON. RGT.	
	11		Battery to rifle range at DICKEBUSCH. Pay parade.	
	12		Physical drills, close order drill, gun drill, interior economy, kit inspection.	
	13		" " Gas-helmet drill. Baths at HOPOUTRE ending. Course of instruction on STOKES 3" to recruits. Work on huts etc.	

Army Form C. 2118.

WAR DIARY
or
INTELLIGENCE SUMMARY.
(Erase heading not required.)

Instructions regarding War Diaries and Intelligence Summaries are contained in F. S. Regs., Part II. and the Staff Manual respectively. Title pages will be prepared in manuscript.

Place	Date	Hour	Summary of Events and Information	Remarks and references to Appendices
DEVONSHIRE LINES.	Dec. 14.		Physical drill. Close order drill. Gun and Gas helmet drill. Route march.	
	15		"	Gun pit inspection &c.
	16		"	
	17		Route march. Work on hutment.	
	18		Church parade. R.C.'s Rifle inspection, respirators.	
	19		Prepared to move to forward area. 'Stand by' order acted upon. Unloaded Carts	
HILL 60 SUB. SECT.	20		Moved to HILL 60 Sub. Sector. Took over from 141 T.M.B. relief complete c. 9.0.p.m.	
	21		Dull. Ammo cleaned. Bomb store received attention. Usual line routine.	
	22.		Usual line work carried on. 'Stood to' in view of raid taking place on night sect-	CABAN S. SECTOR
	23		Gun and Emplacement destroyed by hostile fire. Two positions damaged	
	23		Damaged positions repaired. Line routine.	
	24		"	RAILWAY DUGOUTS
	25		Usual line routine. Work on RAILWAY DUGOUTS.	
	26		" Trench boarding " &c.	
	27.		" T.M.C. dump.	
	29-31		Usual line routine. Work on Emplacements &c.	

Army Form C. 2118.

WAR DIARY
or
INTELLIGENCE SUMMARY.
(Erase heading not required.)

Instructions regarding War Diaries and Intelligence Summaries are contained in F. S. Regs. Part II. and the Staff Manual respectively. Title pages will be prepared in manuscript.

#1 T M Bty

Place	Date	Hour	Summary of Events and Information	Remarks and references to Appendices
HILL 60 SUB-SECTOR	JAN. 1		Heavy hostile bombardment (5.30 a.m – 6.20 p.m) 220 rds fired in retaliation. One mortar knocked slightly damaged.	
	2		Distribution of ammunition. Usual line work carried on. Work on mine area. (RAILWAY DUGOUTS)	
	3		Work on two slightly damaged positions.	"
	4		Usual line work. Sandbagging Hqs dugout. Fitting anti-gas fans to reserve dugouts.	"
	5		— " —	— " —
	6		Drainage work on positions, trenches etc.	
	7		Working party (from reserve section) on new mortar position. Distribution of ammo.	
	8		" (9 rds fired) moved to DEVONSHIRE CAMP	
DEVONSHIRE CAMP.	9		Arrived a. 10.15 p.m. (via DICKEBUSCH). Took over 4 huts	
	10		One hut handed over to 24th LOND. RGT. Clean inspection.	
	11		Physical drills. Route march.	
	12		Snow. Wet. Interior economy. Route march.	
	13		" interfering with outside training. Baths at HOPOUTRE SIDING.	
	14		Frost. Church parade, Work on camp.	

2353 Wt. W25744/1454 700,000 5/15 D. D. & L. A.D.S.S./Forms/C. 2118.

Army Form C. 2118.

WAR DIARY
or
INTELLIGENCE SUMMARY.
(Erase heading not required.)

Instructions regarding War Diaries and Intelligence Summaries are contained in F. S. Regs., Part II. and the Staff Manual respectively. Title pages will be prepared in manuscript.

Place	Date	Hour	Summary of Events and Information	Remarks and references to Appendices
DEVONSHIRE CAMP.	JAN 15		J.M.O. Inspection. Close order drills. Work on Duckboarding etc.	
	16		Close order drill, Gas helmet drill. Haircuts cleaned. Kit inspection etc.	
	17		Wet. Route march.	
	18		"	
	19		Relieved 141 T.M.B. in CANAL SUB-SECTOR. HQS. at CANAL DUGOUTS	
	20		Usual line work. 160 rds fired in retaliation	
	21		Usual work on position etc.	
	22		HQs. moved to WOODCOTE FARM. ditto Battery (from LODGE WALK etc) Usual line work.	
	23/24		Usual line routine. Work on new quarters (reserve)	
	25/26/27		" " " 45 rds fired in retaliation	
	28		" " " Registered from new mortar position	
	29		" " " 45 rds fired in retaliation	
	30		" " " 40 " " "	
	31		" " " 44 " " " 1 O.R. wounded	

KMHHill
Capt.
OC 142 T.M.B.

142nd Trench Mortar Battery

WAR DIARY
or
INTELLIGENCE SUMMARY.
(Erase heading not required.)

Place	Date	Hour	Summary of Events and Information	Remarks and references to Appendices
CANAL SUB-SECTOR	FEB. 1		Usual time routine. HB was first in situation to "Run for activity"	
	2		" "	
	3		Relieved by 140.T.M.B. Moved (at dusk) to Reserve billets (Huts) arr. 9.0.p.m	
DEVONSHIRE LINES	4		Clear up. Inspection. Work in camp.	
	5		Inspection of kit. Interior economy. Gas helmet and close order drill. Route march	
	6		" " " "	
	7		7 guns to Route march	
	8		Baths at HOBOURNE SIDING	
	9/10		Close order drill. Gas drill. Route march. Fatigue party on camp.	
	11		" " " Cleaning of guns	
HILL 60 SUB SECTOR	12		Moved to relieve 141 T.M.B. in Hill 60 Sub sector. Relief complete 7.0.p.m.	
	13		Registration of guns. Line routine. Work on emplacements	
	14		Usual line routine. Situation quiet	
	15/16		" " " Work on new position. Detonating shells at store. 3nd firing	
	17		" " (Registering a) Drainage of position in carried out	
	18		" " Detonating of ammo	

Army Form C. 2118.

WAR DIARY
or
INTELLIGENCE SUMMARY.
(Erase heading not required.)

Instructions regarding War Diaries and Intelligence Summaries are contained in F. S. Regs., Part II. and the Staff Manual respectively. Title pages will be prepared in manuscript.

Place	Date	Hour	Summary of Events and Information	Remarks and references to Appendices
HILL 60 SUB SECTOR	FEB. 19		Line routine work on new positions carried on. 38 rds fired. Amm. prepared.	
	20		Raid by 6th LOYAL REGT. on night we co-operated as laid down in Brigade scheme. 7400 guns on night action manned by us. Two of our guns were temporarily put out of action. 700 rounds expended (as per scheme). No casualties. Work proceeding.	
	21		110 rounds destroyed by shell fire. Work on clearing guns, clearing positions. Carried on. Intersection relief	
	22/24		Line routine. Work on emplacements. } 83 rds fired	
	25/27		"	
	28		Relieved by MG. T.M.B. moved to Devonshire Camp. an c. 9.0 pm (this r-b)	

Army Form C. 2118.

WAR DIARY
or
INTELLIGENCE SUMMARY.
(Erase heading not required.)

142nd T.M. Battery

Place	Date	Hour	Summary of Events and Information	Remarks and references to Appendices
DEVONSHIRE CAMP	MAR. 1		Inspection, close order drill, gas drill. Course of Instruction to reserve section.	
	2		" Route march.	
	3		Physical drill. Baths (at HOPOUTRE siding) Cleaning of mortars "	
	4		Inspection. Church parade.	
	5		Phys. drill. Squad drill. Route march. Party on hut improvement. "	
	6		"	
	7		To line. Relieved 141 T.M.B. in CANAL SUB-SECTOR. Complete 7.0.p.m.	
CANAL SUB-SECTOR	8/10		Line routine.	
	11		" Registration of mortars.	
	12		" Work on emplacements.	
	13		" 60 rounds fired in retaliation to "Pineapple" bombs.	
	14		" 64 " " " " " and T.M.b. 1 O.P. slightly crumped.	
	15/16		" 24 " " " " " Reserve trench strengthened.	
	17		" 30 " " " " "	
	19/20		" H.V. on "Pum Jac" active. 62 rds fired in retaliation.	
	21		" " 33 " " " "	
			" " 50 " " " " One mortar mounted in new position (BRUCE)
			Fairly quiet generally.	
			{Moved to reserve area. DEVONSHIRE CAMP. (K16.1-6) 2.m.	

WAR DIARY
or
INTELLIGENCE SUMMARY.

(Erase heading not required.)

Army Form C. 2118.

Place	Date	Hour	Summary of Events and Information	Remarks and references to Appendices
	1918			
DEVONSHIRE CAMP	22		Clean up. Baths at HALIFAX CAMP. Pay parade.	
	23/25		Moved to Army Training area via STEENVOORDE, ARNEKE. Long wk four guns, ammo etc.	
	25		Arr. GANSPETTE 3.30 p.m. Billet – barn.	
GANSPETTE	26		Clean inspection, Football etc. Billet a fine picquet mounted.	
	27		Running. (Rain prevented) Squad drill, distance judging, route march.	
	28		Weather interfered with O + ⊕ Gun drill.	
	29		Physical drill, squad drill, route march. Football.	
	30		" " " " 9 a.m.	
	31		Running. Bayonet fighting, route march.	

WAR DIARY
INTELLIGENCE SUMMARY
(Erase heading not required.)

Army Form C. 2118.

142nd T.M. Battery
Vol 1

Place	Date	Hour	Summary of Events and Information	Remarks and references to Appendices
GANSPETTE	APRIL 1		Battery Sports. Church parade.	
	2		Snow. Route march.	
	3		Practice firing. Barrage and hurricane bombardment practices.	
	4		Bayonet fighting, physical drill, semaphore exercise, route march.	
	5		Brigade attack practice. (Stokes mortars used.)	
	6		Bayonet fighting, semaphore drill, box helmet drill, gun drill.	
	7		Brigade attack practice No 2.	
	8		Left GANSPETTE. (142. INF. BDE. Opn. Order. 162.) by road to OCHTEZEELE. (arr. 2:40. p.m.) Heavy gear to f.f.	
	9		Left OCHTEZEELE " " " " (" 11:45. a.m.) carried by lorry	
STEENVOORDE	10		" STEENVOORDE. (" 11:45. a.m.)	Sk. Ris. tre.
	11		Clean up. Rifle inspection etc. Pay parade.	
			Left STEENVOORDE. (142 INF. BDE. Ok. Order. 164) to DEVONSHIRE CAMP.	
DEVONSHIRE 12				
CAMP	13/14		Batts. relieved 140 T.M.B. in CANAL SUB-SECTOR and 2 guns in SPOIL BANK SECTION.	
CANAL SUB-SECT.	14	10:10 a.m.	Situation generally quiet. Guns, ammo and emplacement overhauled.	
	15		25 rds fired on small raiding party against 'B' crater. 24 rounds in retaliatory fire against 'Stabsbombe'	
	16		Fairly quiet. About line routine.	

Army Form C. 2118.

WAR DIARY
INTELLIGENCE SUMMARY.
(Erase heading not required.)

Instructions regarding War Diaries and Intelligence Summaries are contained in F. S. Regs., Part II. and the Staff Manual respectively. Title pages will be prepared in manuscript.

Place	Date	Hour	Summary of Events and Information	Remarks and references to Appendices
CANAL SUB-SECTOR	APRIL 17		No 1 position put out of action for firing but badly damaged by round fire in retaliation to hostile mortar fire. Work on new emplacement.	
	18		Sit. quiet. Hostile living routine. Work continued on new emplacement.	
	19		" " " "	
	20		" " " "	
	21	9.0 AM 10.0 "	26 rounds fired in retaliation to hostile T.M. activity. whilst enemy attempted to raid ST ELOI SECTOR. Much damage done by his fire. Quiet. Lewis gun mortars mounted in new emplacement NORFOLK TRENCH (SPOIL BANK.)	
	22		Necessary mortars trained on front between WYNDE and HEDGEROW, in view of suspected hostile mine workouts. Special sentry precautions taken.	
	23		Sit. quiet. Usual line routine. Work on emplacements, stores etc. registration.	
	24		60 rounds fired on targets and in retaliation to hostile T.M. fire.	
			Two guns in SPOIL BANK SECTION taken over by 140. T.M.B.	
	25	4.20 a.m.	Enemy attempted to raid, (vicinity RAT ALLEY - RAVINE (BLUFF Sector). Were able to open an immediate hurricane bombardment, firing 285 rounds causing him casualties. (Later) Our THORNE ST. emplacement damaged and PETTICOAT LANE emplacement destroyed - by hostile shell-fire.	
	26		Sit. normal. Work on emplacements etc.	

2353 Wt W2514/1454 700,000 5/15 D. D. & L. A.D.S.S./Forms/C. 2118.

Army Form C. 2118.

WAR DIARY
or
INTELLIGENCE SUMMARY.
(Erase heading not required.)

Instructions regarding War Diaries and Intelligence Summaries are contained in F. S. Regs., Part II. and the Staff Manual respectively. Title pages will be prepared in manuscript.

Place	Date	Hour	Summary of Events and Information	Remarks and references to Appendices
CANAL SUBSECT.	27		Relieved by 141 T.M.B. moved back to HALIFAX CAMP. (Sheet 10 9)	
HALIFAX CAMP.	28		Clean up. Inspection etc.	
	29		Church parade. Pay parade.	
	30.		Inspection, Close order drill, interior economy.	

140th Trench Mortar Battery.
1.5.17.

[signature]
Capt.
O.C. 142. T.M.B.

Army Form C. 2118.

142nd T.M. Battery

WAR DIARY

INTELLIGENCE SUMMARY.

(Erase heading not required.)

Instructions regarding War Diaries and Intelligence Summaries are contained in F.S. Regs., Part II. and the Staff Manual respectively. Title pages will be prepared in manuscript.

Place	Date	Hour	Summary of Events and Information	Remarks and references to Appendices
HALIFAX CAMP (H.14.)	MAY 1		Inspection. Bayonet fighting. Gas helmet. Clearing of guns etc. Corps inspect. Party to line for purpose of detailing T.M. Guns	
	2		Physical training. Gas helmet Route march.	
	3		Close Order drill, Iron-ration inspection. Gas drill. Route march. Party for detonating T.M. line.	
	4		Physical drill. Musketry & manual drill. Route march.	
	5		" " Camp shelled up to 13 cm How.	
	6		" "	
	7		Church Parade	
	8		Rifle firing practice. Digging anti-shell fire slits in neighbourhood of camp.	
	9		Moved to VANCOUVER CAMP (H.14.31 BELGIUM. 28. N.W. 1/20,000.)	
	10		Digging and completing anti-shell fire slits for whole Battery. Bayonet fighting, close order drill, haversacks etc cleaned	
CANAL SUB-SECTOR	11		Moved to CANAL SUB-SECTOR, relieved 141 T.M.B. (1.30 a.m. night 11/12 complete)	
	12		Line routine incl. registration, work on new emplacements.	
	13		45 rounds fire in retaliation to hostile T.M. activity	
	14		Experiments carried out with new T.M. ring charges. Found them satisfactory	
	15/16		50 rounds fired in retaliation etc. Work on new positions	

Army Form C. 2118

WAR DIARY
or
INTELLIGENCE SUMMARY.
(Erase heading not required.)

Instructions regarding War Diaries and Intelligence Summaries are contained in F.S. Regs., Part II. and the Staff Manual respectively. Title pages will be prepared in manuscript.

Place	Date	Hour	Summary of Events and Information	Remarks and references to Appendices
CANAL-SUB-SECTOR	MAY 17		300 rounds fired in general activity provoked by mine-blowing in Hill 60 sector.	
	18		Line routine. Work party dispersed by M.G. at I.34.a.35.80 (a.15 a.m.)	
	19		" Intersectional relief.	
	20		" Work on new emplacements.	
	21/22		Our guns in DRIVE & WYNDE barraged points in enemy front line during progress of raid by 1/24th LOND. REGT. (R. Section CANAL SUB-SECTOR.) Good report by firing. Lero lane guns by raiding party. One emplacement was wrecked, another damaged.	
	23		Relieved by 141 T.M.B. Section S) 1 of 9 sec. to SPOIL-BANK (S.of YPRES-COMINES	*BELGIUM. Sheet 28 N.W. 1/20,000
			CANAL) to man two guns in left sector.	
	24		Arrived H.O. a.m. "OTTAWA CAMP (9.24.)*	
OTTAWA CAMP.	25		Clean up. Baths at HOPOUTRE SIDING (POPERINGHE.)	
	26		Inspection. Interior economy. Kit inspection.	
	27		Church parade. "SPOIL-BANK" section relieved.	
	28/29		Physical drill, gun drill etc. Interior economy.	
	30/31		Bayonet fighting, gas drill, mortar drill.	

[signature]
Capt.
O.C. 142. T.M.B.

149th TRENCH MORTAR BATTERY.
No. 5
Date 1.6.17

Army Form C. 2118.

WAR DIARY
or
INTELLIGENCE SUMMARY.
(Erase heading not required.)

142nd T.M. Battery

Place	Date	Hour	Summary of Events and Information	Remarks and references to Appendices
OTTAWA CAMP	JUNE 1		Relieved 141 T.M.B. in CAVAN SUB-SECTOR.	
CAVAN SUB-SECTOR	2		Those mortars set and registrom west outlier.	
	3		Work on emplacements, registration etc.	
	4	11/5	" " " Preparations complete.	
	6		Kin routine.	
	7		Second Army Offensive of Aberdeen I & II	
	8		having a no power (Ock on forward positions, tomb-stone etc	
	9		Relieved by 141 T.M.B. moved to BLUFF TUNNELS c.6.0.p.m.	
	10/11		Salvage work, work on huts etc.	
WESTOUTRE	12		Moved (2.15 p.m) to HURST PARK CAMP, WESTOUTRE, via cross	
	13		(Interior economy, B.G.C's Inspection.	
	14		Bath. Moved to (near) ECKE (CASTRE.)	
	15		Moved to RACQUINGHEM (7.0.a.m) arri' 9.120. noon	
RACQUIN- GHEM	16		Inspection. Cleaning of Guns etc. Church Parade.	
	17		Inspection. Route march. Musketry etc.	

Army Form C. 2118.

WAR DIARY
or
INTELLIGENCE SUMMARY.
(Erase heading not required.)

Instructions regarding War Diaries and Intelligence Summaries are contained in F. S. Regs., Part II. and the Staff Manual respectively. Title pages will be prepared in manuscript.

Place	Date	Hour	Summary of Events and Information	Remarks and references to Appendices
	JUNE			
PACQUINGHEM	19		Interior economy. Route march. Bathing.	
	20		Inspection. Infantry tr.	
	21/3		Physical and C.O. orders in parade.	
			Lunch parade. Resistance of people attack by Pickenbrom	
	25		Inspection. Route march. Bathing. 21 gun.	
	26		Moved to B.H.Q. and (SERCUS) Gnr. Squire join. (our Pickenbrom...	
			Moved to METEREN at 7.0 a.m. at 7.12 train. (H.Q. or sub. Q.Q.91.)	
(SERCUS)	28		2a.cav. 5.10 am moved to RIDGE WOOD (DICKERBUSCH) " 1941.)	
	29		Inspection. Rifle inspection.	
	30		Physical and inspection. Close order drill. Grenades.	

[signature]
Capt.
O.C. 142 T.M.B.

142ND
TRENCH MORTAR
BATTERY.
No. 6
Date 30.6.16

142 T M Bty Army Form C. 2118.

WAR DIARY
INTELLIGENCE SUMMARY
(Erase heading not required.)

Instructions regarding War Diaries and Intelligence Summaries are contained in F. S. Regs., Part II. and the Staff Manual respectively. Title pages will be prepared in manuscript.

Place	Date	Hour	Summary of Events and Information	Remarks and references to Appendices
RIDGE WOOD VOORMEZEELE	JULY 1		Reserve and routine	
	2/3		Inspection. Bayonet fighting. Close order and gun drill.	
	4/5		Physical and musketry. Class of instruction in "Stokes".	
	6/7		Section drilling. Bomb store at Spoil Bank.	
(RENINGHELST)			Moved to M.I.A.S.C. (Reut 28, S.W. Belgium). Relieved by 140 T.M.B.	
	9		Clean up. Inspection.	
	10		Bathing parade. Pay parade.	
	11		Physical drill. Route march.	
	12/14		Recreation. Cricket. Platoon and close order drill.	
	15		Church parade. Moved to Sector N.9. YPRES - C. sector. Relieved 141 T.M.B.	
	16/17		Line routine. Work on stores, equipment &c. Revue section area.	
	18/21		" "	Obtained lot 90 shells
	22		" "	Lt JOHNSON H.R wounded (shell)
	23/24		" "	
	25		Relieved by 123rd T.M.B. Moved to DRAGON CAMP, WESTOUTRE. Arr 1.30 am. 26 K. July.	
WESTOUTRE	26		Rest. Clean up	

WAR DIARY
INTELLIGENCE SUMMARY

(Erase heading not required.)

Army Form C. 2118.

Place	Date	Hour	Summary of Events and Information	Remarks and references to Appendices
WESTOUTRE	JULY 27		Inspection. Gun drill.	
	28		" Instruction on 'Stokes' Batt.	
	29.		Church parade.	
	30.		Inspection. Physical Course of Instruction for recruits. Gas drill.	
	31.		" " " General instruction.	

AEFermth 2/Lt.
O.C. 142. T.M.B.

142ND TRENCH MORTAR BATTERY.
No. 7
Date 31.7.17.

WAR DIARY
INTELLIGENCE SUMMARY
(Erase heading not required.)

Army Form C. 2118.

142nd T.M. Battery

Place	Date	Hour	Summary of Events and Information	Remarks and references to Appendices
WESTOUTRE (ABEELE CAMP)	AUG. 2/3		Inspection. Instruction to recruits. Physical drill.	
	4		Physical drill. Route march.	
	5		do. Route March arrive to recruits.	
	6		Church parade.	
	7/8		Physical drill. Route march.	
			do.	
	9	8.45 am	Gun drill. Instruction. Cleaning of guns, carts etc. Inspection.	
			Moved to training area at MORINGHEM. By road to ABEELE. By train to ST OMER. By road to MORINGHEM. Arrived 6.20 p.m. Billeted in town.	
MORINGHEM	10		Physical drill. Inspection. Gas helmet drill. Instruction in use of compass, maps etc.	
	11		do. Route march. Gas mere judging.	
	12		Church parades.	
	13		Physical, Close order and Gun drills.	
	14		do. Army Commander's Inspection.	
	15		do. Report writing. Route march. Distance judging.	
	16		do. Firing practice. Semaphore drill.	
	17	2.0 p.m.	Moved to WIZERNES, entrained for HOPOUTRE (POPERINGHE) & on to Dominion Camp.	

Army Form C. 2118.

WAR DIARY
INTELLIGENCE SUMMARY.
(Erase heading not required.)

Place	Date	Hour	Summary of Events and Information	Remarks and references to Appendices
	AUG.			
DOMINION CAMP.	18		Vicinity of Camp. Clear of Camp, bombed by hostile aircraft. Moved to PIONEER CAMP AREA.	
PIONEER CAMP	19/23		Battery in support. Cleaning up. Inspection. Physical drill. Gas drill. Instruction.	
	24		Kit inspection. Sergeant drill.	
	25		Relieved 141. T.M.B. Took over billets at RAMPARTS and INF. BARRACKS, YPRES.	
	26		Usual routine.	
			Working party (7 O.R.) on new water dump 7.30. a.m. 12.30 p.m.	
		p.m.	do. (26 ") filling do.	
	27.		do. (7 ") to finish do.	
	28.		do. (30 ") to carry grenades to forward.	
			do. (7 ") at 6.30. 11.30 a.m. and 2.20 p.m. to build new bomb store.	
	29.		do. (7 ") to finish bomb store (~2.0.p.m.)	
			do. (21 ") to carry ammo. to new store.	
	30.		do. (7 ") do. do.	
	31	p.m.	do. (21 ") to work on water dump (3.30 to 2.0 p.m.).	

O.C. N⁰. 7.T.M.B.

WAR DIARY or INTELLIGENCE SUMMARY

Army Form C. 2118.

142nd Trench Mortar Bty

(Erase heading not required.)

Place	Date	Hour	Summary of Events and Information	Remarks and references to Appendices
YPRES.	SEPT. 1917. 1		Working party fixing water dump.	
	2		Relieved by 7th T.M.B. and back to SCOTTISH LINES. Two journeys with hand-carts.	
SCOTTISH LINES.	3		To move Q.M. Stores from PIONEER CAMP to SCOTTISH LINES.	
	4		Clean up. Cleaning of guns and hand-carts.	
	5		Work on camp. Inspection. Musketry. Gun drill. Pay Parade. Bath.	
	5		Moved to STEENVOORDE WEST AREA. (142 INF. BDE. O.O. 213). Stores moved by lorry.	
STEENVOORDE	6		Physical Drill. Kit inspection. Kit issues.	
	7		do.	
	8		Gun fire (competitive) Gun drill.	
	9		Inspection. Close Order Drill. Gun practice.	
	10		Church Parade. (R.C.'s and C.E.'s)	
	10		Moved to CAVALRY HUTS, DICKEBUSCH (142 INF. BDE. O.O. 214). Stores moved by lorry to PIONEER CAMP AREA. (Relieved 7/4 T.M.B.)	
DICKEBUSCH	11		Inspection. Work on camp. (Anti-aircraft protective measures.) One O.R. "wounded at duty" from anti-balloon shell.	
	12/13		Physical Drill. Work on camp.	
	14		do. do.	

Army Form C. 2118.

WAR DIARY
or
INTELLIGENCE SUMMARY.
(Erase heading not required.)

Instructions regarding War Diaries and Intelligence Summaries are contained in F. S. Regs., Part II. and the Staff Manual respectively. Title pages will be prepared in manuscript.

Place	Date	Hour	Summary of Events and Information	Remarks and references to Appendices
DICKEBUSCH	SEPT 1917. 15		Physical Drill Inspection. Perfector Drill. Cleaning of kits, etc.	
	16		Moved to MIDDENHOEK AREA (143 INF. BDE. O.O. 215) Took over 5 Tents at L.29. c.f.1.	
			(Sketch) Stores moved by Lorry.	
	17		Physical Drill Inspection of Battery	
	18		Moved to ST SYLVESTRE-CAPPEL AREA (143 INF. BDE. O.O. 26) Accommodated in Manne hut	
			Stores moved by Lorry.	
SYLVESTRE CAPPEL.	19		Physical Drill Inspection.	
	20		do do Gun drill.	
	21		Moved to 1st ARMY AREA. E-trained - BAVINCHOVE. Detrained - MAROEUIL. (143 INF. BDE. O.O. 217)	
MAROEUIL	22	a.m. 11.0	Moved by Light Railway to ANZIN ST. AUBIN (corr. 1.0. p.m.)	
ANZIN	23		Church Parade. Soft Parade.	
	24		Relieved 190th T.M.B. in left subsector of Divisional Front. (143 INF. BDE. O.O. 218)	
			6 guns in line, 2 in reserve. Horses sent to ST. CATHERINE by limber.	
	25		Line routine. Hostile M.G. silenced.	
	26		5 rounds fired against hostile T.M.'s. Line routine.	

Army Form C. 2118.

WAR DIARY
or
INTELLIGENCE SUMMARY.
(Erase heading not required.)

Instructions regarding War Diaries and Intelligence Summaries are contained in F. S. Regs., Part II. and the Staff Manual respectively. Title pages will be prepared in manuscript.

Place	Date	Hour	Summary of Events and Information	Remarks and references to Appendices
	SEPT. 1917. 27/28		Line routine. Registration carried out. New emplacements selected and work commenced on same.	
			Reserve section working party to line.	
	29.		Retaliatory fire - 6 rounds against hostile T.M.b. do. do.	
	30.		Mortar mounted in new position. Line routine. do. do.	
			40 rounds fired in retaliation to enemy T.M. and grenade activity.	

M. Ballyhill
Capt.
O.C. 142. T.M.B.

142ND
TRENCH MORTAR
BATTERY.
No. 7.
Date 30.9.17.

Army Form C. 2118.

WAR DIARY

INTELLIGENCE SUMMARY

(Erase heading not required.)

142nd T.M.Bty

Place	Date	Hour	Summary of Events and Information	Remarks and references to Appendices
	OCT.			
(OPPY Sector.)	1.		Line routine. Work on new positions. 1 mortar mounted in new position. (B.12.a.55.85)	
	2		do. 12 rds fired in retaliation to E.T.M. activity. Registration	
	3		do. Improvement to Positions etc. 7 rds retaliatory fire.	
	4/5		do. 10 rds fired.	
	6		do. Mortars mounted in new positions. (B.24.b.67.) & (B.12.c.95.50)	
	7		do. Registration. } do. 16 rds fired.	
	8		do. } do.	
	9		do. 4 retaliatory rds fired.	
	10		do. 5 } do. (E.T.M's very active). Relieved by 140. T.M.B.	
ST. ANZIN	11.		2.30.p.m. hove in to billets at ST. ANZIN	
	12		Clean inspection.	
	13		Inspection. Cleaning of guns etc. Pay Parade. Baths. Winter clokes issued.	
	14		do. Kit case and inspection. Class of instruction (recruits) Close Order drill..	
	15		Church Parade.	
	16		Physical drill. Inspection. Lecture on map and compass reading	
			do Class of Instruction.	

Army Form C. 2118.

WAR DIARY
or
INTELLIGENCE SUMMARY.
(Erase heading not required.)

Instructions regarding War Diaries and Intelligence Summaries are contained in F. S. Regs., Part II. and the Staff Manual respectively. Title pages will be prepared in manuscript.

Place	Date	Hour	Summary of Events and Information	Remarks and references to Appendices
ST. ANZIN	Oct. 17		Physical drill. Examination in STOKES of recruits. Gas helmet inspection, drill. Pay Parade. Close order drills.	
	18		Relieved 142 T.M.B. in RIGHT (OWN) SUB-SECTOR. Moved to reserve area by lorry.	
(GAVRELLE)	19		Line routine. Registrations checked. 6 r/a fired.	
	20		do. 62 retaliatory rounds fired. Work on bomb stores and emplacements.	
	21		do. 44 do.	
	22		do. 83 do. Three new emplacements completed.	
	23		do. 104 do.	
	24		do. 18 do.	
	25		do. 105 do. E.M.W. and Granatenwerfer activity	
	26		do. 58 do. do.	
	27		do. 50 do. do.	
	28		do. 68 do. (48 of which during progress of raid on RIGHT.)	
	29		do. 97 do. and registration.	
	30		do. 73 do. E.T.M. activity (G.W. and L.M.W.)	
	31		do. 15 do. do.	

R. M. [signature] — Capt.
O.C. 142. T.M.B.

142ND TRENCH MORTAR BATTERY.

Army Form C. 2118.

142nd Trench Mortar Batt'y

WAR DIARY
or
INTELLIGENCE SUMMARY

(Erase heading not required.)

Instructions regarding War Diaries and Intelligence Summaries are contained in F. S. Regs., Part II. and the Staff Manual respectively. Title pages will be prepared in manuscript.

Place	Date	Hour	Summary of Events and Information	Remarks and references to Appendices
(GAVRELLE)	NOV. 1/2		Line routine. Work on emplacement, bomb-stores etc. 34 rounds fired.	
	3		do. do. 110 rounds fired.	
	4		do. do. 1973 rounds fired during progress of raid by 142 Inf. Bde.	
	5		do. Relieved by 141 T.M.B. Batt'y Battery moved to ANZIN.	
ANZIN	6/12		Training. Physical drill, close-order and gun drill. Instructions etc.	
	13		Relieved 140 and 141 T.M.B's on Divl. front. 8 guns manned.	
GAVRELLE OPPY	14/18		Usual line routine. Work on gun emplacements. Registration of ammunition.	
	19		Relieved by 9th T.M.B. Half battery to immediate support, Half in way to St Catherines.	
ST CATHERINES	20		Clean up. Baths. Support half-battery moved to ST CATHERINES.	
MT. ST. ELOI	21		Moved to KLONDYKE CAMP, MT. ST. ELOI (arr. 2.0 pm) Stores etc by light railway.	
BERNEVILLE	22		Moved to BERNEVILLE (arr. 1.45 pm) Stores etc by lorry	
	23		Inspections, equipment, respirators, Lewis gun etc.	
	24		Moved to GOMMECOURT (arr 3.0 pm) Gear by lorry. Billeted in tents.	
	25		Moved to BARASTRE (arr. 7.30 pm) do " huts	
	26		Clean up, inspections etc.	
	27		Moved to BEAUMETZ - lez- CAMBRAI. Gear took over truck from 99 T.M.B. (infy Bde)	

Army Form C. 2118.

WAR DIARY
or
INTELLIGENCE SUMMARY.
(Erase heading not required.)

Instructions regarding War Diaries and Intelligence Summaries are contained in F. S. Regs., Part II. and the Staff Manual respectively. Title pages will be prepared in manuscript.

Place	Date	Hour	Summary of Events and Information	Remarks and references to Appendices
BEAUMETZ lez-CAMBRAI	Nov. 28. 29/30		Physical drills, Rapid gun drills, Box respirator drills. General inspection.	

Sgd J. Ruxton Lieut.
OC 142 T.M.B.

14th D
TRENCH MORTAR
BATTERY

Army Form C. 2118.

WAR DIARY
INTELLIGENCE SUMMARY.
(Erase heading not required.)

Instructions regarding War Diaries and Intelligence Summaries are contained in F. S. Regs., Part II. and the Staff Manual respectively. Title pages will be prepared in manuscript.

Place	Date	Hour	Summary of Events and Information	Remarks and references to Appendices
BEAUMETZ lez CAMBRAI	DEC. 1		Inspection of Battery Guns and Carts cleaned.	
	2/5		" Physical Drill, Box respirator drills, C.O. Drill.	
	6		Battery employed as Ammunition Carrying Party, to forward area.	
	7		do. do.	
	8		do. do.	
	9		Moved forward to HINDENBURG LINE, for immediate support, as required.	
	10/11		In " "	
	12		" "	
(NEUVILLE)	13/5		Relieved by 99 K. T.M.B. Detail (4 O.R.) left as Detonating Party at HAVRINCOURT. Moved to Transport Lines near NEUVILLE.	
	16		Clean Inspection, Close-order drills etc. Moved to railhead VELU. By train to AVELUY. By road to HÉRÉNCOURT. (Somme) Housed in barn.	
HÉRÉNCOURT	17/22		Inspections. Interior economy. Route marches. Clearing of roads and billet approaches of others.	
	23		" Church Parade.	
	24		"	
	25		Battery High tea, Xmas Dinner etc.	

Army Form C. 2118.

WAR DIARY
INTELLIGENCE SUMMARY.
(Erase heading not required.)

Place	Date	Hour	Summary of Events and Information	Remarks and references to Appendices
HENEN-COURT.	DEC. 26/29		Battery Inspections et Tactical exercises et.	
	30/		Road to Railhead, ALBERT. By train to ROCQUIGNY. By road to P.1. CAMP. ETRI-	
	31.		COURT. (Housed in Tents.)	

142ND TRENCH MORTAR BATTERY.

R.M.W.
O.C. 142 T.M.B.

WAR DIARY
INTELLIGENCE SUMMARY
(Erase heading not required.)

Army Form C. 2118.

142ND TRENCH MORTAR BATTERY

Place	Date 1918	Hour	Summary of Events and Information	Remarks and references to Appendices
	JAN. 1		Moved to SAULCOURT WOOD CAMP (LECHELLE AREA)	
	3		Moved to HAMES CAMP, HAVRINCOURT WOOD. Housed in Tents.	
	4		Relieved 58 L.T.M.B. (FLESQUIERES SECTOR) 4 guns in positions the guns & personnel at RIBECOURT. Reserve section housed in catacombs, RIBECOURT.	
FLESQUIERES SECTOR	7		Line routine. Checked barrage and S.O.S. lines. Defensive positions worked on.	
	9/11		No weather conditions permitted. Inter-section relief.	
	12		Line routine. Two moves from advanced (outpost) positions.	
	13		Relieved by 110/M T.M.B. Moved to billets at BERTINCOURT. (overnight)	
BERTIN-COURT	13/15		Clean up. Interior economy. Refitting preparatory to attending course at III RD. CORPS T.M. SCHOOL. General inspections.	
	16		Moved to Railhead YPRES. Entrained with 12 hand-carts and stores by rail to SAULTY STA. (via AMIENS, ROMESCAMPS en-) to HUMBER CAMPS (there)	
	18		CORPS T.M. SCHOOL.	
HUMBER CAMPS	19/30		Attended Course of Instruction on Light Trench Mortars (III RD CORPS SCHOOL).	
	31		En route to OM. 142 INF. BDE.	

OC 142 TMB

WAR DIARY
INTELLIGENCE SUMMARY

Army Form C. 2118.

Place	Date	Hour	Summary of Events and Information	Remarks and references to Appendices
	1918. FEB. 1.		En route to rejoin 142 INF BDE (from III Bo CORPS TM SCHOOL)	
	2		Arrived ROCQUIGNY. Obtained covered tarpaulin to move to BERTINCOURT. Unloaded wagons	
			at ROCQUIGNY etc. Six men sent to store the Bn trestles in huts at BERTINCOURT	
BERTINCOURT	3		Clean up. Inspection of Battery	
	4		Clearing of gun woodwork	
	5		Fatigue party on new playing field	
	8		Moved to training field (BRED) via High Railway to TRESCAULT. By road	
			to FLESQUIÈRES RIGHT SECTOR. Relieved 141 TMB. Began setting in of GARRISONS	
			sub	
FLESQUIÈRES 9/10 RIGHT S.3.			RIBECOURT. 4 guns in position + in reserve	
	11		Line routine. Work on emplacements, dumps stores	
	12		Not connected on No.6 position. No.5 position completed. Line routine	
	13		do	
	14		No.2 gun mounted and manned.	
	15		Intersection? relig. No.6 gun mounted. Old manned line routine	
	16/17		Ammunition brought to replenish forward stores. do	
	18		Line routine. Usual work on dugouts ammunition emplacements	
			do. Shelter for personnel at the positions completed	

Army Form C. 2118.

WAR DIARY
or
INTELLIGENCE SUMMARY.
(Erase heading not required.)

Instructions regarding War Diaries and Intelligence Summaries are contained in F. S. Regs., Part II. and the Staff Manual respectively. Title pages will be prepared in manuscript.

Place	Date	Hour	Summary of Events and Information	Remarks and references to Appendices
	Feb.			
	22		Relieved by HQ TMB. Proceed to BERTICOURT.	
BERTICOURT	23		Moved to ROCQUIGNY (B. Coy) housed in huts	
ROCQUIGNY	24		Church Parade (C.E. R.C. O.C.)	
	25		Interior economy. Gun drill. Pay parade.	
	26		Physical drill. Inspection. Gun drill.	
	27		do. do. Close-order drill. Gun drill. Baths.	
	28		do. Inspection of kit, equipment, clothes. Gun drill.	

142ND TRENCH MORTAR BATTERY.

142nd Inf.Bde.
47th Div.

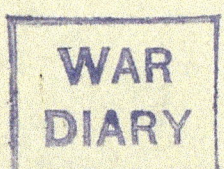

142nd TRENCH MORTAR BATTERY.

M A R C H

1 9 1 8

WAR DIARY
or
INTELLIGENCE SUMMARY.

(Erase heading not required.)

Army Form C. 2118.

Place	Date	Hour	Summary of Events and Information	Remarks and references to Appendices
ROCQUIGNY	MAR 1-15		"DETAILS LOST. ORDINARY REST AREA ROUTINE, TRAINING etc.	
do	16		Battery Inspection. Close order Drill, Musketry	
do	17		Church Parade. Afternoon - Football cup tie	
do	18		Battery Inspection. Range Firing	
do	19		Physical Drill, Gas Helmet Drill, Musketry	
do	20		Move to EQUANCOURT	
EQUANCOURT	21		German offensive opens. Move in evening to CHESTER CAMP near NEVILLE	P.30d. Sheet 51c
NEVILLE	22		Party reconnoitre METZ SWITCH System. Camp shelled by H.V. Guns	
do	23		Receive orders to move to MANNENCOURT. Leave CHESTER CAMP about midday. Battery caught on road between YTRES STATION and ETRICOURT by M.G. fire. Casualties - 1 Killed, 2 wounded. Battery forced to abandon convoy and make its way to BUS. Receive orders to join waggon lines. Move to LESBOEUFS.	
LESBOEUFS	24		Shelled by H.V. Gun. Move with transport to LONGUEVAL. Move about 3 p.m. to CORTOLMAISON. Bombed by E.A. Move on to field behind ALBERT.	
ALBERT	25		Morning move to field in front of MILLENCOURT. Remain few days.	

WAR DIARY
Army Form C. 2118.

Instructions regarding War Diaries and Intelligence Summaries are contained in F. S. Regs., Part II. and the Staff Manual respectively. Title pages will be prepared in manuscript.

WAR DIARY
or
INTELLIGENCE SUMMARY.
(Erase heading not required.)

Place	Date	Hour	Summary of Events and Information	Remarks and references to Appendices
	MAR			
MILLENCOURT	26		Move about 2 a.m. to SENLIS via HENNENCOURT. Afternoon move to VAUCHELLES.	
VAUCHELLES	27		Move to Huts W. of TOUTENCOURT.	
TOUTENCOURT	28		Battery paid out.	
do	29		Move about 6 p.m. to WARLOY	
WARLOY	30		Change over Gellets with 140 T.M.B.	
do	31	11 am	Inspection. Fighting Order. Fatigue work in Billets.	

1.4.1918

[signature] Capt.
O.C. 142 T.M.B.

142nd Brigade.
47th Division.

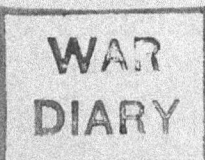

142ndT TRENCH MORTAR BATTERY

APRIL 19-18

Army Form C. 2118.

WAR DIARY
INTELLIGENCE SUMMARY
(Erase heading not required.)

42nd T.M. By

Place	Date	Hour	Summary of Events and Information	Remarks and references to Appendices
	APRIL			
WARLOY	1		Reconnoissance of forward area. Four Norton positions in offensive position. Moved Guns	
AVELUY WOOD	2		forward and prepared same.	
	3/4		Further work on emplacements. Ammo &c	
	5		*Forward Area - Situation fairly quiet. R. Guns adjusted and checked lines.	*AVELUY WOOD area
			Enemy very active. Norton "Vengeoet" on S.O.S. lines. Charge position in afternoon	
	6		to maintain barrage. Resistance given to infantry action in afternoon.	
			Reserve half battery moved forward. Ammo by gun, approximated two minutes hurricane	
			bombardment in connection with infantry action.	
	6	c.6.0 p.m.	Hurricane fire in answer to S.O.S. signal. Reinforced infantry in forward line	
			Moved further Ammo forward. No 1. half battery moved back to Reserve lines (WARLOY).	
WARLOY	7		Battery relieved by 106 T.M.B. C.I.O. a.m.	
	8		Both moved (bytroad) to RAINCHEVAL (2 handcarts with all gear) arrived in	
			new area about c. 6.0 p.m.	
RAINCHEVAL	9/10		Inspections. Interior economy	
	11		Moved to MONTRELET via BEAUQUESNE, BONNEVILLE.	
MONTRELET	12		Moved (9.45 am) to BROILLY via BERRYVILLE, FIREUIL. (Halt for midday meal in route)	

A 6945 Wt. W.14422/M.1160 350,000 12/16 D D & L Forms/C/2118/14.

WAR DIARY
or
INTELLIGENCE SUMMARY.
(Erase heading not required.)

Army Form C. 2118.

Place	Date	Hour	Summary of Events and Information	Remarks and references to Appendices
	APRIL			
BRAILLY	13		General Inspection - Kit &c.	
	14		Church Parade	
	15/20		Battery general training - Musketry, Close Order, Physical, Trench Mortar Drills, Field Work &c &c and confce: work.	
	21		Church Parade.	
	22		General training and Trench Mortar Training	
	27			
	28		Church Parade. Bn C.O.'s Parade by Off Chaplain General. Morses with Bole.	
			Transport Group by road to BAUCAMP c. 6.0 p.m. (12 Handcarts with all gear)	
BAUCAMP	29		Moved (H.Q Coy) with Bde Transport Group by road (12 Handcarts with all gear) to WARLOY via ST. OUEN, VIGNACOURT, FLESSELLES, VILLERS BOCAGE, BEAUCOURT Arrived at WARLOY c. 11.30 p.m. (Halt 'en route' for midday meal)	
	30		Rested.	

[signature]
[signature] Capt.
O.C. 142. T.M.B.

142ND
TRENCH MORTAR
BATTERY.
No. —4—
Date 30.12.1917.

Army Form C. 2118.

WAR DIARY
INTELLIGENCE SUMMARY.
(Erase heading not required.)

101st T.M.B.

Instructions regarding War Diaries and Intelligence Summaries are contained in F. S. Regs., Part II. and the Staff Manual respectively. Title pages will be prepared in manuscript.

Place	Date	Hour	Summary of Events and Information	Remarks and references to Appendices
WARLOY	MAY 1.		Took over L. Bar Sub. Sector from S.R. AUST. L.T.M.B. 4 mortars in line, 4 in reserve.	
	2/5		Usual line routine. Situation normal.	
	6		Two (reserve) guns mounted and manned. Two left (Reserve) positions handed over to 160 T.M.B.	
	7		Situation quiet. Inter-section relief.	
	8		do	
			Line routine.	
	9		157 rounds fired in reply to S.O.S. Two mortars moved forward and took part in action by 23 nd LOND. RGT. (11.0.p.m) 60 rounds fired, giving good results.	
	10		Relieved by 141 T.M.B. Moved to reserve billets at WARLOY.	
	11		Clean inspection	
	12		Church Parade. Withdrawal of Winter Clothing.	
	13		Kit Inspections. Saluting Drill.	
	14		Baths. Inspection	
	15		do	
	16		Took over positions in BAIZIEUX System from 175 T.M.B. 6 guns in position and manned. 2 guns in reserve.	
	17/24		Took over defences in BAIZIEUX system — accommodation, positions, bomb stores etc. Drill and Jock Transport.	
WARLOY	24		Handed over to 54 T.M.B. Took over forward positions from 55 T.M.B. 6 guns mounted and manned. 2 guns in reserve. Also 6 Guns Mounted 2 guns in machine.	

Army Form C. 2118.

WAR DIARY
or
INTELLIGENCE SUMMARY.
(Erase heading not required.)

Instructions regarding War Diaries and Intelligence Summaries are contained in F. S. Regs., Part II. and the Staff Manual respectively. Title pages will be prepared in manuscript.

Place	Date	Hour	Summary of Events and Information	Remarks and references to Appendices
	MAY			
	25.		Situation normal. Hostile act and checked on S.O.S. lines. No. 2.3. registered. Enemy artillery very active on forward area during night.	
	26.		Situation quiet. No. 5.6. mortars registered and checked.	
	27/29		Re-distribution of ammunition. Work on board stores ec.	
	30/31.		Work on Reserve Section Accommodation. Work in forward area on alternative positions.	

Capt.
O/C 7 M.B.

WAR DIARY or INTELLIGENCE SUMMARY

Army Form C. 2118.

Place	Date	Hour	Summary of Events and Information	Remarks and references to Appendices
BAZIEUX	JUNE 1		Relieved by 140.T.M.B. Moved to BAZIEUX CHAU. arr. midnight.	
	2		Clean up. Gas drill (6.0 p.m.)	
	3/8		Training (Guard mounting, Lectures, Close Order, Gas, Gun drill, Physical drill, Compass work)	
	9		Took over from 141 in L. Bde S. Sector (Oise Front). 6 mortars in position, 2 in reserve.	
	10/14		Line routine. Work on new positions. Work on mortars for Reserve action.	
	15		Work on new advanced MBs. 2 mortars mounted on night flank.	
	16		do.	
	17		Line routine. Fired # 180 rds during raid made by 22nd Batt.	
	18		do.	
	19		do. 10 " (retaliatory fire) Transport driver wounded (shell fire)	
	19/20 night		Relieved by 173. T.M. Battery.	
	20		Moved via BAZIEUX to CHAU. MONTIGNY. arr. am. 5.0. am.	
	21		Q.M. Stores and Transport moved to MONTIGNY.	
	22		do. do. by road to OISY. Battery HQ. do.	
OISY	23		Clean up. Pay Parade.	
	24		C.E. R.C. Parades.	
	25/26		Physical Drill, Inspection. 80% Battery inoculated.	
	27/30		Physical Drill, Inspection, Gas, Gun, Close order, Route march, Cricket, Lectures etc.	

142ND TRENCH MORTAR BATTERY.
-6-
Date: 1.7.198.

WAR DIARY or INTELLIGENCE SUMMARY

Army Form C. 2118.

141 T.M. By

Place	Date	Hour	Summary of Events and Information	Remarks and references to Appendices
OSSY	JULY 1/6		General training. Firing demonstrations. Field work.	
	7		Church Parade. Brigade Gymkhana.	
	8/11		Training. Field work &c.	
	12		Moved to forward area. Entrained 11.30 a.m. – to VADENCOURT. Took over from 55 K TMB in L. sub-sector, I. Div. Front, III Corps. Reserve section at MAZE (Sheet 57 D.S.W. – V.24.a.)	
	13/14		Depôt at BAIZIEUX. (8 mortars in position)	
	15		Line routine. Work on positions, ammunition and new emplacements.	
	16/18		Depôt moved to VADENCOURT WOOD. Line routine.	
			Line routine. S.O.S. lines checked and tested.	
			Relieved by 140 TMB. Moved to billets at WARLOY.	
WARLOY	19/20		Clean inspections. Interior economy. Pay parade.	
	21		Church Parade. Baths.	
	22/23		Physical Drill. C.O. Drill. Kit inspection. Gun Drill.	
	24		Relieved 141 T.M.B. in R. Sub-sector. Div. Front. (6 mortars in position 2 in reserve)	
	25		Line routine. Reserve section in HENENCOURT.	
	26		Extension of Div. Front. Took over L. Sub-sector 58 Div. Front. (175 T.M.B.) Our mortars in positions, four in reserve. Handed over to 140 T.M.B. positions &c. in old R. sub-sector 147 K. Div. Front.	

Army Form C. 2118.

WAR DIARY
or
INTELLIGENCE SUMMARY.
(Erase heading not required.)

(14) Trench

Place	Date	Hour	Summary of Events and Information	Remarks and references to Appendices
	JULY			
	27/28		Line routine. Distribution of amm. work on emplacements, and new positions.	
	29.		do	
	30		do 15 American soldiers attached for Instruction.	
			All mortars re-laid and checked. Usual line worked.	

M.R.Nall
Capt.
O.C. 142 T.M.B.

142ND TRENCH MORTAR BATTERY
1.8.1918.

142nd Bde.
47th Div.

142nd TRENCH MORTAR BATTERY.

AUGUST 1918.

142 Trench Mortar Battery

Army Form C. 2118.

WAR DIARY
— of —
INTELLIGENCE SUMMARY
(Erase heading not required.)

Instructions regarding War Diaries and Intelligence Summaries are contained in F. S. Regs., Part II. and the Staff Manual respectively. Title pages will be prepared in manuscript.

Place	Date	Hour	Summary of Events and Information	Remarks and references to Appendices
ALBERT Sector	AUG. 1.		Attached party of Americans returned to Regtl. Duty. General line work.	
	2		Enemy withdrew from first and second line. do	
	3		Small reconnoitring parties proceed into ALBERT. do	
	4		General line work. Work on collecting and re-boxing ammunition.	
	5		Battery relieved by 140 T.M.B. Moved back to machine hills at WARLOY	
WARLOY	6/9		General training. Interior economy. Inspections.	
	10		Buses taken over by SS T.M.B. (18th Divn.) Moved by march route to LAHOUSSOYE.	
	11		Moved forward to Old British Front Line System. (N. of MORLANCOURT.) Took over accommodation from 130 AMER. INF. (in J.11.a. square.) In CORPS Reserve.	
	12		Relieved 175 T.M.B. (58th Divn.) in RIGHT Sector of CORPS Front. HQrs in K.26. square (Sheet 62.D.)	
	13.		Salvage work. Working party on positions in forward area. Two mortars a.d	
	14		do do do	
	15		do Teams taken forward and established in positions prepared.	
	16		Relieved by 140 T.M.B. Moved back into support area in J.11.a.	
	17/18		Inspections, gas drills.	
	19		Working party to work on new trenches in K.10.a.	

WAR DIARY
or
INTELLIGENCE SUMMARY.

(Erase heading not required.)

Army Form C. 2118.

Place	Date	Hour	Summary of Events and Information	Remarks and references to Appendices
HEILLY	Aug. 20		Moved back to HEILLY area	
	21		33 O.R's sick. 10 Lewis guns attached to Battery. Formed a Brigade Reserve Force (2 Officers & 88 O.R's) in Five Platoons. Prepared for re attack.	
	22	12.30 am	Moved by march route (BRAY - CORBIE road) to assembly area in Brit. Second system. Subjected to disturbing shell (H.E. and gas) during attack by French.	Appendix No. 1.
			Advance chened (N.W. of BRAY to ALBERT) Strong resistance by enemy in woods HAILEY sector. Two platoons of Reserve Force moved up about 2.0 pm to close a gap in infantry. No 3 Platoon to O.B.L. on RIGHT. (to support protecting flank) Reserve Force to BOIS d'TAILLES reinforcements. Stood by for orders. Subjected to severe H.E. and Gas shell. 18 O.R's wounded.	
	23		Relieved by 17th LON. REGT. Assembled at BOIS d'TAILLES - moved back (in small parties) to J.I.f.8.I Accommodation taken in trenches.	
	24		Attached party returned to Reg't. Duty. (Passes to CORPS Reserve)	
	25		Moved to CEMETERY COPSE. Attached to R.E. for work on D.H.Q.	
	26		Work on D.H.Q.	
	27		Moved and rejoined Brigade near B. d'TAILLES. Bivouaced in Railway Cutting.	
	28		Moved to HARDECOURT.	

Army Form C. 2118.

WAR DIARY
or
INTELLIGENCE SUMMARY.
(Erase heading not required.)

Place	Date	Hour	Summary of Events and Information	Remarks and references to Appendices
HARDECOURT	Aug. 30		Brigade moved through 35TH. BDE. (12TH. DIVN.) One mortar to forward area. Remainder of Battery moved to MAUREPAS STA. Valley.	
	31		Lorry with 6 mortars and ammo forward to ARDERLU WOOD (N. of LE FORÊT.) Built positions and mounted mortars in B.S.A. (62C Sheet.) Trained on PRIEZ FARM. (1 O.R. killed)	

14280
TRENCH MORTAR
BATTERY.
No. — L —
Date 6.9.16

O.C. 142 T.M.B.

Appendix No. 1. to War Diary Aug. 1918.

(O.R.2)

Synopsis of Action taken in recent operations by 142 T.M.Bty

On Aug 21st 1918 - the 142 T.M.B. formed a Brigade Reserve Company to assist if necessary in the operations. Three platoons were formed comprising 1 officer and 30 O.R's to No 1 and 2 with 4 Lewis Guns each platoon, and No. 3 under command of the Battery Sergeant Major with 28 O.R's and 2 Lewis Guns.

The Company moved to Assembly Area at K.19.a (Sheet 62 D NE) forming up in trenches to the rear of 23rd BATT. The Company moved one hour after Zero to occupy the O.B. system and occupied the trenches in K.12.a. Moved about 11 a.m. into the valley in K.18. About 2.0 p.m. two platoons were ordered to reinforce the 24th BATT. No 1 and 2 Platoons proceeded forward but on arrival in forward area found our troops retiring on the left. The platoons joined up with the 22nd BATT and succeeded in closing a gap on the Right of the 142. Inf Bde. The enemy who was endeavouring to work his way forward was dispersed by Lewis Gun fire. The platoons proceeded to dig themselves in and to consolidate a line of shell holes. The platoons were relieved by the 17th BATT. during the night & the company returned to trenches in J.17.a.

142 Trench Mortar Battery

Army Form C. 2118.

WAR DIARY
or
INTELLIGENCE SUMMARY.
(Erase heading not required.)

Instructions regarding War Diaries and Intelligence Summaries are contained in F. S. Regs., Part II. and the Staff Manual respectively. Title pages will be prepared in manuscript.

Place	Date	Hour	Summary of Events and Information	Remarks and references to Appendices
	SEPT. 1		Front 4000 yds O - Left flank of front, and PRIEZ FARM. Infantry went forward on the RIGHT. Enemy still holding out to LEFT of the farm commanding the valley	Attach /N°2.
	2/3.		Moved forward a rifle section with one mortar and effected capture of 1 Officer 130 ORs. 15 machine-guns.	
			Moved with mortars and ammo. (lorries) to near BEAUCHEVESNES. Battery moved up to ST. PIERRE VAAST WOOD. 2 mortars and ammo. to assist in clearing M.G. posts. About C.6. e.f.6.6. Found to have been evacuated by enemy. Withdrew the two mortars and personnel to Battery HQs.	
	4		18th Div. took over accomodation in WOOD. Battery moved to vicinity of Rav. B.D.E. REPORT CENTRE. C.15.6. (N.E. of BOUCHEVESNES.)	
	5		Stood by.	
	6	am	Moved forward to MURLU (via MOISLAINS.) Bivouaced in WILLE WOOD.	
		8.0 pm	Moved back to old area near BOUCHEVESNES. Forward area taken over by 58th Divn.	
	7		Moved back to Transport Lines at CLERY-sur-SOMME.	
	8		Moved to entraining point. Boarded trucks and de-trucked at MÉRICOURT-L'ABBÉ Bivouaced here the night.	
			(Passed to XIII Corps. FIFTH ARMY)	

Army Form C. 2118.

WAR DIARY
or
INTELLIGENCE SUMMARY.
(Erase heading not required.)

Instructions regarding War Diaries and Intelligence Summaries are contained in F. S. Regs., Part II. and the Staff Manual respectively. Title pages will be prepared in manuscript.

Place	Date	Hour	Summary of Events and Information	Remarks and references to Appendices
	SEPT.			
MERICOURT	9/10		Entrained - to detrain at LILLERS, by march route to ECQUEDECQUES arr. 7.0. a.m.	
ECQUEDECQUES	11		Inspections.	
	12		Moved by march route to ALLOUAGNE.	
ALLOUAGNE	13/14		Training. Interior economy.	
	15		Church Parade.	
	16/18		General training and L.T.M. work.	
	19		Moved by march route to ANTIN (nr. VALHUON)	
ANTIN	20/21		General training	
	22		Quiet day.	
	23/25		General and specialist training	
	26		do. Brigade sports.	
	27		Moved by march route, via ST. POL, to PRONAY	
PRONAY	28		Inspection. Physical and G.O. Drills &c.	
	29		Quiet day.	
	30		Inspection. Physical Drills, Close order drills, Musketry and Gun Drills	

142ND TRENCH MORTAR BATTERY.

[signature]
O.C. 142 T.M.B.

(O R 4)   Appendix No 2. to War Diary Sept 1918
        142 T.M.B.
        SUMMARY of OPERATIONS
        from 5.30 a.m. to 4.0 p.m. Sept 1st 1918

At Zero hour we fired 400 rounds of 3 in STOKES shells into the area of Prey Farm. Reconnoitring party of 3 Officers and 4 O.R's following our attacking troops into Prey Farm, found attack completely successful. Numerous Germans killed and Machine Guns knocked out by Stokes fire. In one place alone a group of four hostile Machine Guns were found with crews dead and guns demolished by Stokes Shells.

The ridge N.W. of the Farm, in T.30.c and B.6.a. was found to be strongly held by hostile machine guns and there appeared to be no defensive flank thrown out. We organised a defensive flank running along trench B.6.a.0.6. to B.6.a.78. consisting of our own battery, one Stokes Gun, infantry detachment comprising of 22nd and 23rd LOND REGT and in conjunction with M.Gs. and some troops of the 18th DIV. After careful reconnaissance we located the enemy nests of M.Gs. Heavy M.G. and rifle fire was carried out on the ridge and we eventually obtained superiority of fire. The enemy was forced to surrender and we collected 1 officer, 130 other ranks who were sent to the cage.

It is reported that in taking the enemy we released a number of the 18th DIV. who had been just recently captured.

Army Form C. 2118.

WAR DIARY
or
INTELLIGENCE SUMMARY.
(Erase heading not required.)

Place	Date	Hour	Summary of Events and Information	Remarks and references to Appendices
PRONAY	OCT. 1		Usual hours programs carried out. gas drill, close order drill in Battery, killed at PRONAY	
	2		Entrained at St Pol. Detrained LESTREM & billeted for night.	
	3		Moved by march route to billets N.E. of LAVENTIE	
	4		Moved by march route to FROMELLES and relieved 59 Division. No guns sent forward.	
FROMELLES	5		Front line reconnoitred by Battery Officers	
	6		Sent 2 guns forward which were put in position to bombard STATION HOUSE RADINGHAM	
	7		Ordinary line routine.	
	8/M		Sgt. RIDDY A.E. awarded the Military Medal. Suffered raid by R. 152	
	9		Bn LONDON REGT & fired a successful burst of 150 rounds on suspected enemy gun position.	
			Enemy commenced his intermittent Battery Headquarters at Reserve Section moved to vicinity of Chateau de Flaches. Headquarters opened at 17.00 at the Spur.	
RADINGHAM	15		At about 17.30 the round section under S.M. JOHNSON received a direct hit from enemy 5.9 intermittens Hycd on the cross roads at RADINGHAM. The following casualties were sustained. 7 killed 6 died of wounds 8 wounded all of 142 T.M.B. also 2 Brigade Signallers who were passing the scene were killed.	

WAR DIARY
or
INTELLIGENCE SUMMARY.
(Erase heading not required.)

Army Form C. 2118.

Place	Date	Hour	Summary of Events and Information	Remarks and references to Appendices
RADINGHEM	15		Our Casualties included 5 N.C.Os dead.	
	16		Battery remained in reserve	
	17		Relieved by 57th Division. Moved by march route to FROMELLES & thence by railway	
			to BOUT DEVILLE	
	18		Moved by march route to BOURECQ	
BOURECQ	19		Day spent in clearing up general smartening up	
	20/24		Training, parties carried out. Physical & "Topographical" Inspection & casting for work	
	25		Class of Instruction of 24 ORs departed for duty. Dr Watts DJ and Capt	
			Hazelwood AVM received history near the Divisional Commander.	
	26		2/Lt Lane J awarded bar to Military Cross. Battery moved by march route	
			to FILLERS STATION entrained for DON from which place marched by road	
			to LOOS outside LILLE	
LOOS	27		General cleaning up in view of march through LILLE on following day	
	28		Took part in march through LILLE or Genl Birdwood officially took the City	
			and occupied billets at HELLEMES.	
TRENCH MORTAR BATTERY. HELLEMES Date 31.10.1918	29/31		Usual training Programme carried out	

O.C 142 T.M.B

WAR DIARY
~~INTELLIGENCE SUMMARY~~

(Erase heading not required.)

Army Form C. 2118.

Instructions regarding War Diaries and Intelligence Summaries are contained in F. S. Regs., Part II. and the Staff Manual respectively. Title pages will be prepared in manuscript.

Place	Date	Hour	Summary of Events and Information	Remarks and references to Appendices
WILLEMS.	1918 Nov 1		Battery moved from HELLEMES to WILLEMS by march route	
	2		Battery training	
	3		Church Parade, Baptismal Service at Church	
	4/6		Normal training carried out	
TEMPLEUVE	7		Battery HQs moved to TEMPLEUVE. Divnl HQs to PONT-A-CHIN and relief of 141 T M Bty completed by 2000 hrs. 5 hours panel ride from Normal line routine	
KAIN.	8		Normal line routine	
	9		Battery HQs moved by march south to PONT-A-CHIN. Battery concentrated in village. Moved at 1700 hrs to KAIN.	
FRASNES	10		Moved by march route to FRASNES. Enroute filled up craters & cut down trees at MONT ST AUBERT to enable transport of Bn Division to proceed	
KAIN	11		Returned by march route to KAIN. On route were received Armistice order	
	12/13		Normal Billet routine	
TOURNAI	14		Moved by march route to TOURNAI. Command of Prisoners of War Camp (Allied Repatriation) taken over. 2000 returned prisoners consisting of	

A0945 Wt. W14422/M1160. 350000 12/16 D. D. & L. Forms/C/2118/14.

Army Form C. 2118.

WAR DIARY
or
INTELLIGENCE SUMMARY.
(Erase heading not required.)

Place	Date	Hour	Summary of Events and Information	Remarks and references to Appendices
TOURNAI	1918 Nov 14		Retired first Italian retaliation halted during occupying of R.R.	
	15/22		Sort at Tournai & no long carried on — two routes by full rolls	
CYSOING	23		Moved by march route to CYSOING	
	24		Rested	
HAUBOURDIN	25		Moved by march route to HAUBOURDIN	
BETHUNE	26		Moved by march route to BETHUNE	
ALLOUAGNE	27		Moved by march route to ALLOUAGNE. Services billets taken over	
	28/30		Normal Reserve training	

M W Held
Capt.
O.C. 142 T.M. Bty.

WAR DIARY
or
INTELLIGENCE SUMMARY.
(Erase heading not required.)

Army Form C. 2118.

Place	Date	Hour	Summary of Events and Information	Remarks and references to Appendices
ALLOUAGNE	Dec 1916		Quiet Day	
	2		Musketry exercises on Range. Sports	
	3/5		Usual Reserve training. Sports	
	6		Bathing Parade	
	7		Usual training programme carried out	
	8		General cleaning	
	9		Sports. Church Service	
	10/12		Physical exercises, gun cleaning, Limber washing. Lecture	
	13		Musketry Exercises on Range. Route march. Lecture	
	14		Bathing Parades. Instructional classes. Sports	
	15		Physical Exercises & Sports. Lecture	
	16		Church Services	
	17/21		Musketry on Range. Limber washing. Sports	
	22		Aeronautical Short. Usual training programme. Sports	
	23/31		Church Services	
			Usual training programme.	

O.C. 142 T.M.B.

www.ingramcontent.com/pod-product-compliance
Lightning Source LLC
Chambersburg PA
CBHW081557160426
43191CB00011B/1960